THE COMFO...

NEW
REVISED & EXTENDED
VERSION

WRITTEN
&
ILLUSTRATED
BY

JUDAH JAH LOVE

THE
COMFORTER

NEW EXTENDED VERSION FROM
JUDAH JAH LOVE

LOVELIGHT
Publications ©

ISBN 978-1-9997018-8-8

New Extended Version, 2nd Edition © 2018

THE

COMFORTER

For
me ole pa, Rick,
my angel-queen, Khabi
and our baby princess, KaRa,
you all bless my life so beautifully.
xxx
Also for my mum, Sandy, who
has always been there
for us all.
x

"...no one of existing things doth perish,
but men in error speak of their changes
as destructions and as deaths."
– From Chapter 8 of The Corpus Hermeticum

Contents

List Of Figures

Introduction

Greetings in the name of Life, Love and Truth. If you are reading this book having lost someone, I'm so, so sorry, it's *horrible,* I know. You probably don't want to sit down and read a whole book right now, so I've highlighted 12 passages throughout the book in bold capitals which encapsulate the book's overall message, which can be found compiled together on P.112, so you can read them first if you wish, which could help bring you quicker comfort. Hence, **I HAVE CALLED THIS BOOK, "THE COMFORTER," AS I BRING YOU GOOD NEWS; THAT ETERNAL LIFE IS AUTOMATIC AND IS FOR EVERYONE. IN THIS BOOK, I WILL SHARE WITH YOU MY OWN PERSONAL EXPERIENCES AND REVELATIONS ABOUT LIFE WHICH HAVE HELPED MY FRIENDS, FAMILY, STRANGERS AND MYSELF DURING THE DIFFICULT TIMES OF LOSS – MY HOPE IS THAT THEY HELP YOU TOO.**

This book is not based on my, or any particular religion, as truth applies to *everyone.* It's not my intention to force any religious or spiritual views onto you, but rather to relate to you my own true experiences and understanding of the reality of eternal life, with the hope of giving you a new perspective that helps you get through the sad times of grief. This is not a lengthy book, as I try to share, in as much of a nutshell as I can, the things that I have come to believe, to the point of knowing, which have
given me a completely different perspective on life,

1

helping me understand the reality of what has actually happened when I have "lost" relatives. I say "lost" in inverted commas because this perspective sees that death is not the end of our life and that we don't actually lose anyone.

I'm not talking about reincarnation, although reincarnation does seem to be a reality for many. Neither do I simply mean that the dead live on in our hearts, in our memories or through their children. I'm talking about the fact that LIFE LITERALLY HAS NO END; that we don't die along with our bodies; that what we were before we were born is what we will be again when the flesh dies. The after-life is not the *next* life, it's the *original* life, so the traditional *con*cepts of birth and death no longer exist in my imagination as they are misleading, for birth is not the beginning of life... neither is death the end of it.

Our physical life is but a moment in our eternal existence, making it so precious that we should not let anything or anyone – including ourselves – prevent us from living our lives happily and with love. Be happy, even if you are suffering – for because of that suffering, good things are coming to you as long as you live and think positively, for the nature of life depends on the fairness of balance. Always trust that good will be victorious; that love always conquers evil and that life always conquers death. Don't focus on the surface, because that is too sad, too unjust and it will only bring more pain. No, look deeper. Look beyond the flesh, beyond limitation. There is no limit to the spirit. Read on... *death dies today.*

2

Chapter 1: Language Of Life

Our natural reaction to news of a death is usually to not accept it; to reject it. This is in fact a good response, for what we have been told is an unintentional lie. One that has been perpetuated for too long. Our first instincts are usually spot on, so we should trust them, for death doesn't mean the end of the person's life. We should be careful to re-affirm this in our speech and, in turn, our mind by making sure that everything we say is true and accurate, to keep us from becoming over-sad, for the very words man uses about death depress us. It is what we are told to believe about death that makes us sad, for man does not understand life properly and uses terms and explanations that are bleak and misleading. Ignore the sad illusion and trust your inner feeling.

In fact, there are many words which man uses, like, death, birth, luck, fate, coincidence etc... which limit our understanding and spiritual growth. **THE DICTIONARY'S DEFINITION OF DEATH: "DYING, END OF LIFE; END" – GIVES THE IMPRESSION THAT WHEN OUR BODIES DIE, IT'S ALL OVER, FINISHED. THIS MISCONCEPTION CONTRIBUTES TO OUR SORROW, WHILE GOING AGAINST THE TEACHINGS OF NEARLY <u>EVERY RELIGION OR SPIRITUAL BELIEF SYSTEM IN THE WORLD, BOTH PAST AND PRESENT,</u>** for nearly every culture teaches that faith and good deeds lead to eternal life in a good place.

The saying, "You bring nothing into this world and

take nothing out of it" is another lie, for when we are born into the flesh, we bring our spirit, our mind, our energy, love, happiness and joy into the world and death does not steal these qualities from us, as we retain them along with our knowledge, experiences and memories when we leave this physical world.

So be mindful of the words you use in reference to those who are no longer in flesh. Speak of life only, for death is an illusion. Words carry energy. They carry vibrational powers that have an effect on the material and emotional planes. We must then beware of using the wrong words or having the wrong ideas or beliefs about life so as to avoid worsening negative emotions or experiences. They say the truth shall set us free, so we should let it do so, by reminding one's self of the truth at all times. And what is that truth? That things are not what they seem; that the flesh distracts us from the truth by its limitations and its perspective; THAT DEATH IS FAR FROM BEING THE END OF THE LIFE FOR OUR LOVED ONES.

Our speech must always keep the light of this truth shining brightly in our minds, so **I DO NOT SAY, "REST IN PEACE" AS WHEN THEY ARE FREE FROM THE FLESH, THEY HAVE NO NEED TO REST, IN FACT THEY BECOME INVIGORATED WITH THE LIMITLESS ENERGY OF LIFE, NO LONGER RESTRICTED BY THE FLAWS OF THE FLESH, SUCH AS FATIGUE, DISEASE, DISABILITY OR OLD AGE. NEITHER DO I SAY THINGS LIKE "I LOVED THEM SO MUCH," BECAUSE THEY ARE *STILL* ALIVE AND I *STILL* LOVE THEM, JUST AS THEY STILL**

LOVE ME. Our relatives wont stop loving us just because their body died, for love doesn't let a technicality like invisibility get in its way. Society encourages us to use past tense to refer to our "lost" loved ones. We are advised to let go of them and accept that they are gone, when in fact *they are only gone from sight* – things that are not material do not reflect light, so we can't see them, but this does not mean they are not there.

So, as you will see, our biggest problem is our perspective of things and it is this that causes a large bulk of our pain and sorrow. That's why I wrote this book; to change our perspective of life and death; to replace bleak pessimism with radiant optimism and to free the universal gift of eternal life from the confines of any one religion to everyone and everything.

For me, R.I.P. stands for "Restored In Perfection," because the spirit of the person whose body has died has returned to it's former, youthful, fully–able state, as the flesh–death is actually a spiritual renewal. So I shall no longer use the word "death," but "restoration" instead. The word "death" should only be used in reference to a body.

Restoration is not something that should be feared or allowed to tear our lives apart, as it really isn't the end of life. When my dad left the flesh, I found myself not eating, not bathing and crying all the time. Even though I knew the truth of the message of this book – that "there's no end to life or love" – I still found it such a difficult period of my life. The world seemed to be a completely different place, with such a huge hole in it. However, in time, I cried less and less and my life gradually returned to normal, as yours will too, trust me.

What I share with you in this book has made my return to normality that much easier and quicker than it seems to take many other people because it has given me a completely new perspective of life, that allows me to carry on with my life in confidence and comfort. I'm sure you're a good person and you deserve to be happy instead of feeling pain and sadness. I HOPE THIS BOOK GIVES YOU THE UNDERSTANDING, COMFORT AND STRENGTH TO GET YOU THROUGH THE DIFFICULT TIMES AND, EVENTUALLY, HELP YOU LIVE YOUR LIFE TO THE FULL, REGARDLESS OF WHAT THIS LIFE THROWS AT YOU.

Chapter 2: I Have A Dream

You may be wondering what I mean by saying those who have left the flesh are still alive – and how I could know this? Well, what follows are two revelations I've had about the nature of the reality which follows the death of the flesh, which came from dreams/visions that let me *feel and experience the truth.*

Many people have dreams where they are about to die but wake up just before it happens. It is said that if you die in the dream, you don't wake up – this is not true. I know this because I had a dream where I was falling from a building and hit the ground and died, yet I'm still here to tell the tale, so some dreams are real and others are spiritual night classes. As I hit the ground, I felt a sensation at the back of my head, but it wasn't pain because it came and went before I could really feel it. The next thing I knew, I was back in the air and weightless. I said to myself, "I must have just died... but... I'm still thinking to myself." I became aware that although I had died, I was still conscious, still aware... *still me!*

It was this that led me to the realization that *the mind survives the body's death* and that the mind is where our spirit resides, which is why I refer to the soul as the spirit-mind. The mind is not a material object, it's more like a place; the place where our spirit, our true self, resides.

What is not physical cannot be destroyed,

therefore the mind and all that is contained therein does not perish with the flesh. We all have an image of ourselves in our mind – that mental "you" can never die, as we don't need a body to think, for we think with the mind, not the brain. The brain receives the mind-waves; it is the telephone that keeps the spirit communicating with the flesh, but it does not contain the mind, as you cannot confine that which is immaterial and eternal. The mind is bigger than the body and the spirit-mind is sort of anchored to the body, by the ego's identification with the flesh, until the body falls away from it, allowing it to be free again.

Now you could say that it was just a dream and that dreams aren't real, but for me, it was as real as real feels. Besides, the undeniable clarity and common-sense of the dream's magnificent message are what matters most. Granted, some dreams are just dreams, but some are real visions. Having said that, both visions *and* dreams can have several real purposes; for example, while this dream taught me what I believe to be the truth about the state of reality immediately after the death of the flesh, it also served to help someone I know.

There used to be a Jamaican record shop, hidden away down a quiet side street, away from the hustle and bustle of Tottenham High Road, where you could find some reggae gems and even more priceless characters – beaming dreadlocked youths and youthful elders dressed sharp, sipping Cock's Spur rum and stepping gracefully to the sounds of the Island.

The owner was usually an ever-smiling Rasta Man,

8

always speaking words of positivity and humour, but this particular day he did not seem his usual self. It transpired that his brother had just passed away and so I told him about the dream I'd had and relief seemed to wash across his face. It was as if I had been sent there to tell him about my dream, because his brother had committed suicide by jumping off a building and it was especially comforting for him to hear that the pain would have been over before his brother even felt it. He needed to get this message and it was delivered (remember I said "coincidence" is another one of those misleading terms; a "myth-interpretation" if you will).

[One little note about suicide, while it has been mentioned, is that suicide is not the fast track to Hell as it has been made out to be. I know this, as the bulk of my proof of life existing beyond the death of the flesh comes from signs given to me by my dad, who took the life of his own body due to depression. The physical life of sufferers of depression appears to be more Hellish than Hell itself, which kind of makes me understand why my dad did what he did if being alive was such an unbearable torment. Being angry at someone for doing this is normal, but we shouldn't hold on to that anger, nor should we blame ourselves or take it personally, as they have most likely experienced something that has put them out of their right mind (more on "mental ill health" later), preventing them from thinking rationally in that moment. My dad was/is a good man, always trying to help someone. I don't think he realized *just how much* he would be missed, or how much his leaving would hurt so many. Suicide completely devastates the friends and family of the victim, whilst robbing the victim of the chance of experiencing the beautiful side to their life, for something good was always coming to them to balance out their pain. This is why it is so important for us to keep faith in love conquering all. We must *all* stay strong. PLEASE HOLD ON. DON'T GIVE UP.]

My second revelation of there being no end to life came in the form of a real dream-vision. About two weeks after my dad had left the flesh, he came to me in a vision, which began with an image of my late-aunty, Doris. I was aware that I was seeing my dad after he had "died" and I was so pleased to see him. I put my hand on his shoulder – which I could actually feel – and said, "It's so good to see you," and we talked for a while. When I woke up, I was in floods of tears, but as I gradually calmed down, I became aware of a song playing in my head. It was Leona Lewis singing, "Some people wait a lifetime for a moment like this." How true. Usually, we have to wait 'til the end of our physical lives before we can see our "lost" loved ones again, but I had just been blessed with the experience early.

I was so moved by my vision that I thought I should call my mum, Sandy, and tell her about it, but, when I checked the time it was 6:30 a.m. and I didn't want to wake her. Later that morning my phone rang. It was mum – "Did you see him last night?" were her first, emotion-filled, anxious words. "Yeeeees!" I replied, with the strongest feelings of amazement, joy, surprise and relief all at the same time. "Oh good" she said, "I thought you did, because he came to see me last night and you were with him."

10

Mum said that, in her dream-vision, she told me I could talk to my dad, but apparently I struggled to speak because there was so much I wanted to say, but didn't know where to begin. At that moment he turned to me and said, "I know." He already knew everything I wanted to say to him as his spirit-mind had returned to its Source, which is all-knowing (more on this later). As I'm sure you can imagine, this gave us both an immeasurable amount of comfort, but there's even more; as if to prove beyond any doubt that what we had experienced was real and to add weight to a message already hard to deny, the day we had the dream-visions turned out to be dad's mum's birthday (my nan had left the flesh the year before). This link also told me that mother and son had been re-united. Beautiful.

My girlfriend, Khabi (Bokhabinyana), had "lost" her dad not long after I had "lost" mine (although we hadn't met at that time) and I asked her if she'd had any dreams about him. She hadn't. Some weeks later, it was Father's Day and I took her to my dad's body's grave, where we placed flowers for both our dads, as her dad's body is buried in Africa. We poured a drink of spirits for our dad's spirits, blessed them and prayed.

The next day, Khabi told me that she'd seen her dad in a dream that night. She said he simply looked at her, put his hand on her shoulder and smiled. Then she woke up. It was only a moment, but it was a priceless, *real* moment and it comforted her. She tells me that since then, things have become easier to cope with as it was enough to let her know that he is okay where he is now.

11

The dreams we all had, the date of the dreams, the hand on the shoulder in both mine and my girlfriend's dreams shows you that this is not mere coincidence; that life and love really are eternal; that somewhere beyond the flesh there is a continuation of existence for those who appear to die.

Chapter 3: Signs Of Life

To celebrate my dad's first birthday since he'd left the flesh, my mum and I went to his body's grave. I only go there for certain occasions or to maintain the grave because I know he sees me do this and it pleases him. However, I do not go there to be near him, or use it as an opportunity to speak to him as I know that he is in a non-material, spiritual/mental dimension, which allows him to be anywhere at any time – even in two places at once – making it possible for me to talk to him and be near him whenever and wherever I want to. When I miss him, I just start talking to him, knowing he hears me.

What makes me so sure he hears or sees me? Well, I'd made a tape of his favourite tunes and played it at the graveside (tunes like "Miss You" by The Rolling Stones, "Return To Innocence" by Enigma and "Running Away" by Bob Marley). I lit some incense and a candle, poured out his favourite drink (Whiskey) and prayed. My mum and I reminisced about some funny memories and good times – it was a really nice experience.

We stayed until it started getting dark and then we got into the car, which was my dad's old car, and began to drive away. As we set off, the interior of the car suddenly lit up! I looked out the rear window, thinking there was a car behind us with its lights on, but there was no car. Then I realized that it was the interior light that had come on, as if by itself. Mum said, "Its Ricky, isn't it, he's saying thank you, isn't he!?!" He used the light to communicate his presence, appreciation and, most importantly, that he is still very much alive.

As if that's not enough, the following year, we went back to the cemetery with Khabi and did all the things we'd done for his previous birthday and, later that night, when Khabi and I were going back to my flat (which was my dad's flat), we got into the lift and pressed the button for our floor. Now, for as long as I can remember, that button has been broken and *never* lit up, but that night, it lit up – another sign of life... in the form of light.

We were shocked and thought maybe it'd been fixed, although this was highly unlikely as my dad's birthday is on Christmas Eve and I don't think there's many electricians out fixing lift buttons on Christmas Eve. We agreed that if it lit up the next day, it must have been fixed. It did not light up. In fact, it hasn't lit up ever since (although, since writing this book, there has been one other time the button lit up... the day I bought Khabi's engagement ring and came back to the flat with it! Dad's blessing, perhaps!?!) So, on both birthdays, my dad gave a sign of life and each time it was a sign of light; hence, at the end of the tunnel... LIGHT.

Not long after my dad's body died, I was at my mum's flat when I suddenly smelled something burning. I began looking around to see if there was anything burning or if there were any windows open, but there was nothing burning and no windows were open. The smell grew stronger and then I recognized it. It was a cigar... my dad would have a cigar at Christmas or New

14

Years and his body died just after New Years. I had never smelled a cigar there before as my parents were long separated. I just knew it was him. Some days later, it happened again and, this time, my mum smelled it too. It's now two years later and we haven't smelled it since.

These experiences let me know that **THE PEOPLE WHO HAVE LEFT THE FLESH REMAIN AMONGST US FOR SOME TIME AND CAN COME AND GO, CHECKING UP ON US FROM TIME TO TIME. THIS IS WHY IT IS IMPORTANT NOT TO LET GRIEF PREVENT US FROM LIVING A NORMAL LIFE, FOR THEY SEE US, HEAR US AND FEEL US; THEY STILL LOVE US AND WANT US TO BE HAPPY.**

You will see and hold your "lost" loved ones again,
I PROMISE.

Be strong. Be patient.

When you realize that their sunset...
...was actually their sunrise,
your dawning shall turn your
mourning
into
morning.

Chapter 4: Define Divine

In this book, I unavoidably refer to "the Creator", even though the book's not about religion, so I think I should take this opportunity to explain exactly what I am referring to when I mention the Creator... She may not be what you'd expect. I will also explain how I know that such exists.

Having grown up in the UK, my religious education centred around Christianity so, although I am not Christian per se, I do quote the Bible because it's simply the religious source I'm most familiar with. I'm sure that there will be equivalents in your own beliefs, for while I believe that Divine Truth is present in the Holy Bible, I do *not* believe that Divine Truth is limited to the Bible or Christianity alone. I know the Bible has been edited and purposely mistranslated, but I trust truth to be like a weed that breaks through the man-made concrete that covers it and reveals itself to light.

The Bible *has* been tampered with, but it *still* contains Truth. For example, if you want to know who edited Psalm 46, then turn to it and count 46 words in; the 46th word is "shake." Then, not including the word "Selah" as it is not present in many versions, count 46 words back from the end of it; you get "spear." Yep, Shakespeare signed "his" Psalm, which proves that there is at least one piece of the Bible that is not completely original in form.

However, the original versions of many other

Biblical Psalms and Proverbs can be found in the Ancient Egyptian book, "The Wisdom of Amenemope," whose obvious similarity to the Bible proves: 1. Parts of the Bible *have* remained unedited for millennia. 2. The so-called myths of the ancient world gain credence and validity by their very inclusion in the Bible. See, also the similarity between the the story of Adam and Eve and the Sumerian story of Ninhursag.

Then there are the things in the Bible that have correlations with actual historical events. The book of Revelations says that one day, during a great battle, there would be someone with the name "King of Kings and Lord of Lords... Conquering Lion of the tribe of Judah," who would be triumphant. This could well refer to the fact that Haile Selassie I, a direct descendant of Solomon (like Jesus) was crowned in 1930, King of Kings, Lord of Lords, Conquering Lion of the tribe of Judah and protected His country from Mussolini, whose intentions were to colonise Ethiopia, knowing that She houses the Biblical Ark of the Covenant, which would have been his ultimate prize.

The fact that the Bible prophecies so precisely match historical events confirms it contains at least some portion of truth. The Creator is all-knowing and would not have bestowed the Bible upon us if He thought it would be rendered useless by man's vain attempts to limit others, for a sense of superiority and control. This does not mean that I believe that other non-Bible-based religions are wrong. Quite the opposite in fact, as I have come to the realization that *there is Divine Truth running*

18

through all religions (by religion I mean any system of belief that is about worshipping the Source of all life, the Divine Good), *for Truth is religiously inconfinable due to its universality.*

My good friend/brother, Shaun once related this reasoning to me; True religion is like pure, colourless light that, when shone through a crystal, it gives you all the colours of the rainbow. These different colours are the different religions of the world, coming from one original light. I think that this makes perfect sense as *one* God created *all* people, of *all* religions. If God condemned you for being, say Jewish or Muslim, then He wouldn't create people in those countries where you are bound to become one of these – that would just be sick.

There are so many similarities amongst religions because the Truth is universal and, because it has been revealed to so many different cultures in various ages, it has acquired many different labels. The fact that there are many similarities between Jesus, Osiris and Dionysus does not mean one has been copied from the other, making one right and the others wrong, it just means that the same Truth has been revealed more than once, in different places, in different languages. Just look at images of the Virgin Mary with Jesus and see how similar they are to images of Isis with Horus (see Figure 1, P.82).

We are all simply trying to connect with the Universal Source of all life, yet most people will say that if you do not belong to the "right" religion, you will not be saved.

19

My belief is that *if you genuinely desire to find and love the Creator, you are already saved* – even if you end up looking in the "wrong" places, for He/She/It will know your intention and will love and save you all the same, as long as you are doing what you feel and know to be good and right.

The truth is, God is Love and Love is not partial or judgemental. Love is all-embracing and, like truth, it is universal and constant. Even the non-believer unknowingly believes in God by believing in Love. We must stop limiting ourselves – and God – by thinking that one religion is right and all the others are wrong and therefore everyone else is going to Hell. This is the very vanity that does not please the Creator of ALL life.

We must stop trying to divide one from another. We must stop trying to elevate ourselves above others and stop pointing out the differences between us and, instead, focus on what we have in common. This is the righteous attitude of loving humanity unconditionally, hence the Bible says that God advises us to, **"Love one another, as I have loved you."**

Why do I believe that a Creator exists at all? First, let us look at the biggest argument against the existence of God; evolution. Evolution is used to argue that all life-forms developed naturally from the simple amoeba by chance or accident. Yet I believe we were created with intention and with love. Now I'm not saying evolution didn't happen, I'm saying that evolution *and* Creation happened. Man uses evolution to drive a wedge between

God and Man, but God used evolution to drive the act of Creation. Who said a natural process like evolution couldn't be a purposeful act?

The evolution of plants and animals was set in motion by the Creator. This was followed by the *separate, intentional* Creation of human beings, who have also evolved from their first appearance to how they look today. Look at how human life grows from a tadpole-like sperm, to become a foetus, then a baby, then an adult. During this process, we undergo many physical changes and end up looking nothing like how we started out. Surely this is an evolution of sorts. Humans even appear to still be evolving, for we are bigger than we were just a couple of hundred years ago; look at the doors of old houses and antique clothing and you'll see how much smaller we were, not so long ago.

Evolution is like when a gardener plants a seed and the seed changes form as it grows, forming roots and a stem. It buds and flowers and produces leaves and fruits that have a purpose – to sustain living creatures. This, in itself, is a form of evolution set in motion with purpose, for the tree and its fruit look nothing like the seed it sprang from. Yet the gardener knew exactly how the seed would look when fully grown and what fruit it would bear.
He watches over it and tends to it when needed. He provides all the right conditions for its growth, making sure it gets enough light and water. Just because the process of growth and change occurs naturally, it does not rule out the existence of the gardener (in the Bible,

God is the first Gardener as He created the Garden of Eden).

"But evolution goes against religion," I hear you cry. But does it? The Qur'an says that life came from the water, which science has proved to be correct, giving us another religion – Islam – implying that some sort of evolution must have taken place. The Bible also talks of the evolution of life from the water in Genesis 1, verse 20, where the Creator said, "Let the waters bring forth abundantly the moving creature that hath life, and fowl that may fly above the earth", so we now have two very different religions saying the same things – that evolution happened... and that *God made* it happen.

The waters brought forth creatures and birds. Surely this is evolution. Surely it doesn't mean that the birds came flying out of the water. It was evolution set in motion by the Creator. Now we can answer the age-old question, "What came first, the chicken or the egg?" First we must define the egg as a chickens egg. Then, it has to be the chicken that came first, because chicken eggs come from chickens. Where did the chicken come from? It came from the egg of its ancient predecessor – probably a chicken-like bird, which ultimately evolved from a fish, like everything else did.

<u>Evolution does not disprove Creation, for *evolution is the process of Creation.*</u> So, Darwin's theory is only half right. If evolution was the only process bringing forth life, then how come so many flowers rely on bees to reproduce? One of the bee's reasons for being is to

pollinate the flowers. They were made for each other, otherwise there would only be self-pollinating flowers in existence. Even the flowers are coloured to attract the bees. How would the flowers know bees even existed to begin to try to attract them or become reliant upon them?

Speaking of insects, there are some that, for protection, are perfectly shaped and coloured to look like the leaves that surround them – how, if not by intent? You could say "natural selection," but that would only go as far as explaining the accuracy of their resemblance to leaves, but it doesn't explain how they came to look like leaves in the first place. They certainly didn't think, "Hmm, it would be really handy if we looked like leaves!" and then proceeded to have leaf-like babies. Nature is so perfect that it has to be the work of a Creator.

Science is often used to argue against the existence of a Creator, but it can only go so far. For example, I watched an hour long documentary about how water appeared on the planet. The conclusion was that all the Earth's seas, oceans and springs etc... were originally one huge blob, floating about in space which just happened to pass by the Earth, whose gravity pulled it down onto Earth, which just so happened to be the only planet close
enough to the sun to prevent the water from turning to ice, while being far away enough from the sun not to make the water boil. Is it me, or does this sound a bit far fetched? Surely God, "the Cosmic Gardener" simply watered His garden.

Before God created the animals and people, He

created grass and herbs. Why? Because they are medicine and food for animals and humans alike. Are we to believe that herbs just happen to have a positive effect on our health? [For all you vegetarians out there, the Bible says, in Genesis 1, verse 29, that the herbs and fruits shall be for man's meat. Also, in Proverbs 15, verse 17, it says, "Better is a dinner of herbs where love is, than a stalled ox and hatred therewith."]

Okay, lets get down to the nitty gritty; Who and What is God? Well, the Bible says in Saint John, Chapter 1, verse 1, that, "In the beginning was the Word, and the Word was with God, and the Word was God." What was that Word? Well, in Hindu religion, everything was created from the Word, or sound, Aum (see Figure 2, P.84). However, before the Word was pronounced, there must have been the *Thought* of the Word – the Thought of the Word must have already existed in the Mind of God. Here Is the answer; God is Mind. It is from this Mind that all things spring into being: Mind into matter (see Figure 3, P.85). It is from this Divine Mind that our minds come from, or exist in, as they never completely leave their Source.

So far, we have seen evidence of six religions – Hinduism, Rastafari, Ancient Egyptian religion, Christianity, Islam and Judaism – that contain Divine Truths. All of these agree that water played a part in the Creation of life. The Bible goes on to say, in Genesis 1, verse 26, that, "God said, Let us make man in our image,after our likeness." So, although evolution has occurred, we were never monkeys. We were always a separate species, which is why the missing link has not been found – there isn't one.

Even if, one day, a missing link was to be found, it still wouldn't mean that the process of evolution was an unintentional occurrence. Some will bring up the fact that human DNA closely resembles the DNA of the African Ape, but this just proves that the materials used to make humans came from the same source as the materials used to make the African Ape. Man was made from the earth, the black clay that Egypt was named after, "Kemet" or "Kham" ("Ham" in the Bible means "black"). Man was made from the materials already present in the world.

Man was made in God's image in the Garden of Eden. The Bible says that Ethiopia was part of the garden of Eden in Genesis 2, verse 13, and the oldest human remains were found in Ethiopia, so it follows that the image of God must resemble that of an Ethiopian (hence Rastafarians worship an Ethiopian God). That said, however, this could only refer to the image of God the Father, as in the Holy Trinity of Father, Son and Holy Spirit. Why? Because, for God to have a form/image, then He must also have a Former/Imaginer... God Himself must have a Creator.

Who, or *What*, could possibly be the Creator of God? In the Christian concept, God is a Trinity of Father Son and Spirit (Father, Mother and Son in Egypt). The Father and Son are one and the same – see Saint John 10, verse 30, where Jesus says, "I and the Father are

One." This leaves us with the Holy Spirit; The Holy Spirit is the shapeless, nameless, colourless, birthless, deathless and ageless Mind of God, which must have created God the Father and Son, who, in Tri-unity, created everything else. This identifies the *Most High* God as being the Holy Spirit... THE HOLY SPIRITESS; the female element of the Holy Trinity; the Mother of God, Queen of Heaven; it was She who created God the Father and the Son.

God Almighty is Father and Son, the Divine Masculine, while the Most High God(dess) is the Holy Spirit, the Divine Feminine, sometimes called Sophia, "Wisdom," or Venus. I believe this is why we find the so-called "Venus figurines" (see Figure 4, P.86) all over the world, dating from nearly 40,000 years ago to relatively recent times; ancient man worshipped the Divine Feminine. The Ankh, so important to the ancient Egyptians, represents Life, but its symbol is also used to represent Venus – Love (God is Love. God is Life). I believe that this is because they acknowledged that all creation ultimately comes from the Divine Mind, the Sacred Feminine; Love/Venus (see Figure 5, P.88).

The human brain is made of two halves, one male, one female. The male half thinks methodically, while the female half thinks/feels emotionally and is the spiritual half, linked to creativity and psychic ability – hence "women's intuition." The Holy Spirit is made of the type of Mind that is creative, therefore its nature is feminine. This makes the Holy Spirit the feminine aspect of the otherwise male Holy Trinity. The essence of this Mind is

26

Love and Love is creative, which is why our minds and thoughts are creative, for we are created in the image *and likeness* of God. In reference to this, the Bible says in Psalm 82, verse 6 and, in Saint John 10, verse 34, "Ye are gods."

This means we are physical, Earthly representations of God. Mentally, spiritually and physically, we have some of the characteristics and creative abilities of God, for our thoughts can become things. We also have the ability to create life, which in itself is a miracle; making love is making God happen, as it causes the miracle of creation to take place (see Figure 20, P.111). God is Love; God is Mind; God is Goddess; Goddess, the Holy Spirit, is Divine-Love-Mind and is Omnipotent (All-Powerful), Omniscient (All-Knowing) and Omnipresent (Present everywhere); She permeates all life and space, and is constantly with, and within us all (see Figure 7, P.90).

What, then, should we call God? Well, Psalm 68, verse 4, of the King James version of the Bible says, "Sing unto God, sing praises to his name: extol him that rideth upon the Heavens by his name JAH, and rejoice before Him."
However, in more recent versions of the Bible, "his name JAH" has been replaced with, "His name is the Lord" instead. Why has man done this if not to limit our spiritual ability?

Since I began using the name "JAH" in my prayers, I have had good, visible results, because I have faith in it,which is the key to *effective* religion/FAITH. According to the Bible, whenever Jesus healed somebody, He said to them, "<u>By your faith</u>, you are healed." It was *their own faith in their own belief* that brought about the healing, showing that the way we think has an impact on our health and life and the power of our prayers.

I'm not saying that this is the *only* name for God, for that would be placing a limitation on God, confining Him to one language and culture. Every religion in the world is worshipping the *same* Being... the Creator of ALL life... of believers *and* non-alike, it's just that everybody has different names for It. It was explained to me (by a non-Muslim) that every human being has the name "Alla" written in their palms; just put your hands together with inter-locked fingers and look at the pattern the main lines on the palm of your hands make – "Al" on the left and "lA" on the right (see Figure 6, P.89). All humans have these marks on their hands, again showing God's unbiased Nature.

Followers of *all* religions have had prayers answered, so God really doesn't seem to care what religion you are,
as long as you are good. Humans need to get over themselves and stop trying to elevate themselves above others, for any reason. We are all one, with one God, one aim, one destiny, one Source, one life and one love. Religion should not be used as an excuse to make war against others, but rather to *love and unite* with others, for what is not love, is not God/good.

So JAH is the name of God that has been given in

the Bible and has since been purposely obscured by man, but it doesn't refer to the feminine part of the Holy Trinity; the Holy Spirit or Divine Mind. She has been called "Sophia" throughout the ages, hence the word "philo-sophy" relates to matters of the mind (literally the love of Wisdom). So, from here on, I shall refer to God as "JAH-Mind"... JAH being the male parts of the Holy Trinity, and Mind being the Holy Spirit; the female part of the Holy Trinity.

The fact is, though, you can call God whatever your religion calls It and if you don't have a religion, then "The Creative Consciousness", "The Universal Source of Life" or simply, "Love" are all good alternatives. Even "The Inner Divine-Self" can be used, as JAH is within us all, hence the Rastafari term for one's self, "I and I," meaning JAH is part of us all (I, myself and I, Selassie I... God and man as one). JAH is the Brahman within us all – the ultimate destination of the inward spiritual journey, as taught in Yoga, which literally means "God-Communion." The real "you", the true self, is God, hence God is known as "I AM." I am I AM, you are I AM... everything that exists is I AM. [Note: God is I AM and "I am" in French is, "Je suis," so God/"I AM" is "Jesus" and one's self/"I" – Je su(I)s!]

Some say, "If there's a God, why did He let .... die?" Well my point in this book is that *they don't die*, they continue to live outside their body, free of restriction and disease. We must realize that death is not necessarily a punishment, which would help us understand why it seems the good die young.

29

Some also say, "If there's a God, why do bad things happen to good people?" Well, bad things largely happen due to *people, or ourselves,* behaving or thinking the wrong way. Our minds are creative and can materialize that which we concentrate on most; the problem being that we tend to focus more on what we *don't* want to happen, instead of what we *do* want to happen (see, "Living Without Strain" by Dr Joseph Murphy – a brilliant and enlightening book).

We should also bear in mind that all experiences, good *and* bad, are leading us higher in spiritual growth. It is not God's fault that bad things happen, it's man's fault. Even the devil is not to blame, for he doesn't even exist (see, "I Am The Life" by Prof. Murdo MacDonald-Bayne – an amazing, revealing book of truth). Quite often, you will see the devil portrayed as a goat. This has always bothered me, because how could any of nature's beautiful creatures
be associated with anything evil? Then, one day, it just hit me – the devil is the original scape-goat, something for man to blame the results of *his own* wrong doings on, instead of taking responsibility himself. There is no devil. There is no death. There is only Love and life.

Chapter 5: Life After Life

"The body belongs to the Earth
and the Ka (spirit) belongs to Heaven"
– Ancient Egyptian Proverb.

When something has life, it has energy. LIFE IS
THE ENERGY OF THE SPIRIT, WHICH IS LOVE.
SCIENCE TEACHES US THAT ENERGY CANNOT BE
CREATED OR DESTROYED, IT CAN ONLY CHANGE
FROM ONE STATE TO ANOTHER STATE. THIS MEANS
WE LITERALLY HAVE NO BEGINNING AND NO END. WE
ARE ALWAYS ALIVE. We are indestructible, for our real
self is not physical; it is not made manifest in this
physical realm and is therefore untouchable by time,
disease or weapon.

Before we were born into this body of flesh, we
were conscious spirits in our mind, in unity with the Mind
of the Creator. When we were born, our spirit and mind
were delivered into flesh. The flesh we are given is not
our true identity, but a temporary mask. The combination
of our spirit and mind is the true essence of our being
and it is this that survives the death of the flesh, for it is
immaterial and immortal. When we "die", we are spirit-
mind freed from flesh and we then return to our Source
(see Figures 8, 9 and 13, on P.93, 95 and 102). A person
dies, but their personality does not; what we were before
we were born is what we shall be again – our Source is
our Destination (see Figures 10 and 14, P.97 and 104).

IT IS SAID THAT A CIRCLE HAS NO BEGINNING

OR END, BUT THIS IS NOT TRUE. A CIRCLE'S END IS ITS BEGINNING. WHILE THE CIRCLE IS BEING COMPLETED, THE BEGINNING AND END ARE VISIBLE, BUT, ONCE IT'S COMPLETE, END MEETS BEGINNING AND THEY DISAPPEAR. THIS IS THE VERY NATURE OF LIFE. WHEN THE BODY DIES, END MEETS BEGINNING AND, THUS, BEGINNING AND END CANCEL EACH OTHER OUT, FOR THE LIFE AFTER DEATH IS THE SELF-SAME LIFE AS THE ONE BEFORE BIRTH (see Figures 16 and 19, P.106 and 110).

ONCE THE FLESH HAS BEEN SHED, THE SPIRIT-MIND IS FREED FROM THE LAWS AND FLAWS OF THE FLESH, SUCH AS DISABILITY AND DISEASE, AND IS RESTORED TO ITS FORMER GLORY IN PERFECTION, NO LONGER SUBJECT TO CORRUPTION OR LIMITATION AND IS FREE TO BECOME SUBJECT TO ITS OWN IMAGINATION, JUST LIKE IT IS WHEN WE DREAM. ONLY THE BODY DIES, WHILE THE SPIRIT-MIND REMAINS CONSCIOUS AND ALIVE, for the next stage of life is in our mind, where the truly free spirit-mind re-unites with the Mind of the Creator. As it was in the beginning, so shall it be in the end. We have Eternity in Mind, while the flesh-life is fleeting, however long or short it may be (see Figure 11, P.100).

Even animals live on beyond the flesh. When my mum was a child, she had a dog named Lucy, who used to sleep at the bottom of the stairs and she used to have to step over her to get past her. Some time after the dog had been put to sleep at the vets, my mum came down the stairs and saw the dog laying there and she stepped

32

over her as usual. Then she realised the supposed impossibility of what had just happened.

More recently, my mum had been seeing the blurry image of a dog in her flat, out of the corner of her eye (she did not have a dog at that time). Then, one day, a workman was at her flat and he said to her, "I don't mean to scare you, but there's a dog here watching me work!" He went on to explain that he was a psychic medium. Mum asked if it was a black Labrador cross. He said it was and that its name was Peggy. He also said, if she saw Peggy again, to simply tell her to go home.

Then one day a man visited my mum's workplace and said that he lived in her building before it'd been converted into flats. Mum asked him if they'd had a black Labrador cross there called Peggy – they did indeed, but she was actually called Penny. He was so shocked that she knew this. This proves that after this life, there is more life, for everyone, *including* the creatures. For plants, however, this goes without saying, for we see them "die" in the winter and then "come back to life" in the spring (inverted commas here because, in reality, the plants are alive the whole time... just as we are).

My great grandmother, Rosalie, had been suffering from Alzheimer's disease for some years. She was disconnected from the world around her and no longer recognized anyone. One day, my great aunt, Ruby, went to visit her and, to her great surprise, Rosalie recognized her and spoke with her... *Alzheimer's gone*. Suddenly, Rosalie started looking around her and said to Ruby,

"Look, there's George (her son) and there's Lesley (her husband)." She was seeing people who had already been restored.

"Can't you see it?" she asked, "Oh it's so beautiful." Her spirit-mind was leaving her body behind and she was seeing into the next stage of life. Rosalie then fell asleep and her spirit-mind went forward/back to its Source, restored in perfection, back to the the mental reality we all come from and, at the right time, we all return to, re-united with our previously restored loved ones. This shows that "mental ill health" is not forever, while life itself is.

When you are "out of your mind," you are lost in confusion, gone to pieces, so it must follow that when you go into your mind, you are found in perfection, whole and mentally together. When the spirit-mind is free from association with the distracting, corruptible flesh, it is free from all the limitations of the flesh, such as senility or "mental ill health." I use inverted commas here as I know that the mind is not physical and therefore cannot be subject to any kind of defect. Rather the cause of the problems associated with mental ill health must lie within the flesh; the brain. No one's mind is ill, for what is not material cannot be faulty.

Another example of this was revealed to me about H.L, who was a client of mine when I was working as a support worker for adults with learning disabilities. H.L would have, at times, very challenging behaviour and was also beginning to show signs of dementia. He was, however, a great character and I enjoyed working with him. When my dad was restored, I left the job and, not long after that, I heard that H.L's health had started to deteriorate and that he eventually "died."

Some time later, I saw him in a dream-vision. In this vision, we were on a bus and I was aware that I was seeing him even though he was supposed to be dead. I was so pleased to see how well he looked. This was because he is now free from the body of restriction, allowing his mental image of himself to be how he wants it to be. He was dressed very smartly in a suit and he no longer suffered from any of the issues I knew him to have; his speech was clear and he looked fit and strong, just like I always knew he would someday be.

Why did I dream of us being on the bus? It was because in the flesh-life, H.L used to love riding the buses all over London by himself. He is still doing what he loves to do. The bus is of no significance to me, but to him, it means a lot. It's not something I particularly think of when I think of him, so it must have been *him* who thought of the bus and put us on it in the dream, meaning my dream-vision was getting *external influence*, proving the reality of the experience.

When we mourn someone, we are mourning the loss of the flesh, but **THE FLESH IS SIMPLY THE VEHICLE OUR SPIRIT-MIND CHOSE TO FULFILL THE PURPOSE OF ITS VISIT TO EARTH. IT IS ONLY THIS VEHICLE WHICH DIES, NOT THE DRIVER. IF I DROVE IN A CAR TO MEET MY WIFE, SHE WOULD GREET ME**

RATHER THAN THE CAR, FOR IT'S WHAT'S INSIDE
THE CAR THAT IS THE REAL ME. ALSO, IF THE CAR
BREAKS DOWN, I DO NOT BREAK DOWN WITH IT, BUT,
INSTEAD, I GET OUT OF IT AND CONTINUE MY
JOURNEY WITHOUT IT. EVEN THOUGH I MAY BE
ASSOCIATED WITH THE CAR AND EVEN RECOGNIZED
BY IT, IT IS NOT ME. I AM THE DRIVER WITHIN AND I
AM MUCH LONGER-LASTING THAN MY VEHICLE.

Furthermore, I am never *part* of the vehicle (see
Figure 9, P.95), I am a separate entity making use of the
vehicle. It *is* very sad when someone's body dies, but we
must keep reminding ourselves that *it is just the body
that has died* and that the person we love and miss, lives
on. So, when the flesh dies, the spirit-mind is released
into the atmosphere of Earth and can remain amongst us
and see how we are doing, until they decide to, or realize
they are able to fully enter the spiritual, immaterial
reality of the JAH-Mind, still able to check in on us
whenever they feel to, or when they hear/feel us trying
to connect.

This means that, **WHEN WE LOSE SOMEONE, WE
SHOULD BE MINDFUL OF THE FACT THAT THEY ARE
STILL NEAR US, SO WE SHOULD BEHAVE HOW WE
WOULD LIKE THEM TO SEE US BEHAVING, KNOWING
THEY STILL LOVE US AND STILL WANT US TO BE
HAPPY AND MAKE THE MOST OF OUR LIVES. KNOW
THAT AS LONG AS WE ARE HAPPY, THEY ARE HAPPY**,
just like it was before they went from our sight.
NOTHING HAS CHANGED.

However, if they were bad people in this life, then

36

there will be a change, for their mind will be in the presence of Omniscient Mind and free of their ego, meaning they will not be able to deny their conscience and will have to face and feel their own negativity until the desire to be that bad person is utterly gone and they attain their proper positive state of being and thinking.

Negative thinking, behaviour and experience can and should be replaced by positivity now, while still in the flesh-life to prevent us from experiencing further negativity. This will be discussed in Chapter 7. Negative memories and mental scars of past bad situations will be washed away by the tranquillity of the very nature of the environmental reality of JAH-Mind in pure concentration. In blissful meditation, mind becomes totally calm and settled, knowing all things, so we don't need to worry about our restored loved ones, as eternal happiness and unlimited understanding shall be their ultimate reality.

JAH-Mind sees and knows everything as It is present everywhere and is connected to each of our minds; nothing goes unnoticed, so no bad deed shall go unpunished and no good deed shall go unrewarded. Perfect balance. Fairness does exist, for we are, each one of us, connected to each other and we are all connected to the Holy Spirit, meaning that what happens to one, happens to all... and to God. So for injustice and negativity to ultimately succeed in any scenario would mean God has been defeated. This does not happen. Love conquers *all* – and not by force or attack, but by replacing negativity's illusion with its eternal reality.

All who choose to love will enter into the purest

37

form of existence and live eternally in Love's Light. Love is all embracing and always chooses to love, understand and forgive. Love nourishes and enriches. Love is everywhere; it is all encompassing, whether speaking religiously or otherwise. Love can be found anywhere and everywhere. True Love will never let us down. Love is not limited or conditional. Love is not cruel or hurtful. Love is Wisdom, so She didn't spend billions of years, using a network of the gravity and light of a billion more planets and stars to create a place for us to experience a life of independence and apparent individuality, only for us to live for 100 years then vanish into nothing. What a waste of time and energy that would be and Love never wastes Her time (or ours).

Chapter 6: Re: Re-incarnation

WHEN THE SUN GOES DOWN, WE MISS IT, BUT
WE CAN REST ASSURED OF OUR INEVITABLE
REUNION WITH IT, IN THE LIGHT OF THE NEXT DAY.
ONLY WE, WHO ARE LEFT BEHIND, KNOW THE
DARKNESS OF NIGHT, BECAUSE FOR THE SUN ITSELF,
IT IS AN ETERNAL DAY. THIS IS THE TRUE NATURE
OF OUR LIVES. WHEN SOMEONE LEAVES THE FLESH,
THEY ARE ONLY GONE FROM SIGHT, BUT WE DO SEE
THEM AGAIN, IN THE LIGHT; THE SUN WILL NEVER
KNOW NIGHT AND WE SHALL NEVER KNOW DEATH.
So in truth, we lose no one, we only lose sight of them,
temporarily.

Will they be re-incarnated? Possibly, but this
would not mean we wont see them when we get there,
because when they are free of the flesh, they have no
limitations, no restrictions, so they can be in two places
at once. That being true, however, there is also the fact
that time only exists in the physical world, so a short
time between physical lives could in fact be experienced
as many, many years, which means they can and will still
be there even if, in our world of time, they had already
been re-born.

There are many documented stories of re-
incarnation, but the ones that have struck me the most
are as follows: First, there was a documentary on TV
about a girl in Sri Lanka, named Purnima, who from a
very early age claimed that her mum was not her mum;

that she had *another mum* and had another family... when she used to be a boy. When she was a boy, she/he used to sell incense made by his family. She said the name of the incense was the family's name, Ambika. She went on to say that one day, he was out selling incense when he got run over by a bus and died. Her story was investigated and it was found that there was a family, far from where she lived, who made incense and who had lost a son in the way that she had described.

Purnima was taken to meet this family and, although she had never been to that area in her current life, she began to recognize the scenery. While they were driving, she said that there was going to be a large area of water around the corner. Sure enough, there was a large lake around the corner and the family they were looking for lived by its edge. Upon arriving at her "old family's" home, she recognized many of the family members and there were smiles and tears all round. A packet of the incense was brought out and it did indeed bare the name Ambika, but Purnima said that the packaging seemed to be different now – right again.

Finally, a member of her current family lifted her top to reveal a large birth-mark that went right across her body, matching the injury caused by the bus. There was no doubt in anyone's mind; Purnima was their "dead" son. Interestingly, there had been a gap of several years between the boy's "death" and Purnima's "birth", showing that when people do get re-incarnated, it doesn't necessarily happen straight away, nor does it have to be hundreds of years later (see Figure 16, P.106).

40

The other story of re-incarnation that stands out in my memory is also one I saw on TV, where a boy was talking about how he had always been afraid of loud noises, so, to find out what was the cause of this, he went to be hypnotized, to be regressed – taken back in time in his memory. However, his memory went beyond his present life and he began to describe a scenario where he was a soldier holding a gun and could hear the sound of explosions and was scared for his life.

He remembered a lot of detail and drew pictures of his gun, his uniform and the camp he was based in. The boy claimed that he had in fact been an African American (even though he is now white) fighting in the civil war and he could even remember his wife's name. The pictures he had drawn were looked at by experts, who confirmed that everything he had drawn was indeed contemporary to the American civil war. He remembered getting shot in the hand and found that the sound of gunfire was what had brought about the fear of loud noises. Since finding all this out, he has lost his fear of loud noises and has become a drummer in a reggae band.

Re-incarnation is more likely to happen to someone who has had an untimely restoration, such as a fatal accident, cot "death," murder or suicide etc.., or to allow the person another chance to complete any remaining missions/learning they may have, for we have many reasons for being here on Earth.

Our main reason for being is to express and share the Love of JAH-Mind, but we have countless other reasons for being here, such as to help one another when we can; to gain and share knowledge; to make discoveries and many other reasons unique to each individual, so if something happens that prevents us from fulfilling these things, we will keep coming back to Earth until we have done what we came here for.

I believe that a spirit-mind that has completed its Earth mission and progressed to higher states of reality can at any time decide to come back to Earth for any number of reasons. So re-incarnation may well be a reality for many, but I don't think that it is the goal of life to constantly keep coming back to Earth, as this is not progress. Rather, we are meant to keep going forward to higher states of consciousness and re-unite with the Source of our life, the JAH-Mind.

Chapter 7: Dream-Heaven-Reality

Where is Heaven, then, and what is it like? Well, as I have said, the mind survives the body, so Heaven must be in the mind, but it is far from imaginary.

Stories of people "dying" in hospital for a certain amount of time and having memories of seeing themselves and the doctors, or having other "after" life experiences, before being revived, are well documented, *proving that the mind still functions even when the body does not* – this is a most important fact to remember.

Earlier, I spoke about how some dreams are actually real dream-visions. Well, I believe that the place we go to in those dream-visions is of the same nature as Heaven, in that it is a mental reality that can be manipulated by the mind. We can, in theory, "wake up" in a dream and become aware that we are dreaming. When this happens we should be able to have control over what happens in that dream.

I believe the same must go for our Dream-Heaven-Reality. We retain all our senses (in fact, we most probably *gain* senses), even touch, because we remember how things feel and, like I said earlier, I had a dream-vision of my dad, where I could actually feel his shoulder. Heaven is a communal dream reality, with everyone being in the same place, but having different experiences – like this life, but without limitation or suffering.

Beyond the flesh we are still ourselves and still conscious, but we have more ability to control what happens and change our environment or even change our appearance and form in an instant (just like in a dream, where one minute you could be flying, the next minute you're at work in your pyjamas – or is that just me? Anyway, moving on...).

In fact, the possibilities would be endless in a mental reality. We would only be limited by our own imagination or doubt. For example, I once had a dream where I was in the back of a car, which was being driven by my friend, Shaun. His girlfriend, Lisa, was sitting in the front, next to him. I was leaning forward, between the two seats, trying to hear the conversation over the music, but then I realized something... Shaun doesn't drive. "This must be a dream," I said to myself. "Naaah, I'm definitely here." Then I ran a few checks; "I'm breathing, I'm thinking, I can feel the leather seats and I can smell the interior of the car, it must be real," I thought, "*but Shaun doesn't drive*," I said, arguing with myself in my head.

Just then I realized I had no memory of getting into the car, nor did I know where we were going. "OK," I thought, "if this is a dream, I can make this car fly"and with that intention, I felt that feeling you get in your stomach when you're on a plane that's taking off. However, at that same moment, I thought to myself that this is impossible and, guess what, the car did not fly.

Even in a place where anything was possible, I

limited myself by doubt. We can be our own worst enemies when it comes to doubting our abilities or making positive things happen in our lives. We have the ability to bring about positivity, health and success by focusing on such things in our minds and having faith in Good being ever triumphant. Fear and doubt are nothing but a hindrance to us and we must learn to completely let them go from our imagination.

Here is some more good news: YOU DON'T HAVE TO DIE TO GO TO HEAVEN. We must endeavour to always focus on the positive side of things and keep our mind-set happy. By doing this, you enter Heaven while on Earth. I do not believe in the traditional *concepts* of Heaven and Hell; they are not so much places, as mental states (hence the phrase, being "in a good place" means being in a good frame of mind).

Our thought, or state of mind determines the experience we have in this life *and* the spirit-mind life. So, if you're a bad person with bad thoughts and deeds, your mind will become a mental Hell for you, which will be seemingly inescapable, replaying the effects of the bad things you've done over and over until you feel so bad for what you have done that you begin to truly desire to be a better person.

I say that Hell is *seemingly* inescapable due to the fact that it does not have to be forever, in that *if* you realize that what you are doing or thinking is wrong and change your attitude and behaviour, then you can save yourself from yourself, in this life *or* the "next" (inverted

45

commas here because it is not the next life, but a continuation of this life).

A change of heart and mind *now* shall be your quickest salvation.

However, if you're a good person, with good thoughts and deeds, then you are living the righteous life and your mind-set will be optimistic, positive and happy; you will like yourself and others will, too; you are already in Heaven. Some people you know may even call you Angel.

However, you could be a positive person with a Heavenly mind-set, then something could happen, such as a tragedy, that affects the way you think and, in turn, changes your mental Heaven into Hell. This is why we must be careful about how we respond to incidents, events and other people's words and behaviour etc.., so as not to lose our rightful place in Heaven.

For example, when someone brings negativity to you, trying to make you feel angry, sad or ugly, we must be aware that they are seeking a reaction from us and want us to behave in a way that is not like us. If we allow this to happen, then we are giving other people power over us, allowing them to rob us of our positive attitude, effectively stealing our Heaven (remember that the hurtful things people say to you, more often than not, is really how they see themselves, or is what other people have said about them).

Stay in your mental Heaven at all times. Don't let

situations or people get you down, for downwards is Hell-wards, distracting you from your Heavenly birth-right. Whether here in flesh or there in JAH-Mind, mental Heaven can turn into mental Hell and vice-versa, so try to make sure your thoughts are as good as you want your experience to be.

When the body dies, the ego dies too, for the ego gets its power from the flesh – it is fed by it. So once we are free from the flesh and our spirit-mind returns to JAH-Mind, we begin to think truthfully and honestly – one can no longer lie to one's self because the conscience, or rather the inner JAH-Voice, is Omniscient and has been with you all the way through your life.

This means that even if a bad person manages to go through their whole life ignoring their inner JAH-Voice, not changing their ways and seemingly getting away with everything they do, they are heading for a shock, because once their spirit-mind reaches its Source, they will not be able to deny their wickedness and they will experience the bad things they have done and feel the pain that they have caused others. This will go on indefinitely until they come to the realization of exactly how wrong they have been, becoming truly sorry for what they have done, genuinely desiring to be, and becoming, a better person.

Perpetrators become victims of themselves until begging for forgiveness and changing their attitude and behaviour. If they don't do this, then they run the risk of living in that mental Hell forever or simply become caught in the re-incarnation loop (see Figure 12, P.101), experiencing life after life of negativity, until they have a true change of mind.

At that point, I believe that their Hell reality will turn into their Heaven reality, for JAH-Mind is Divine Love, which is ever merciful, ever forgiving and ever loving. This is why the Bible says that we shall be judged by the Son and not the Father, for *we* are the Son (or Daughter) of JAH, our own minds shall judge ours lives. JAH doesn't judge us as JAH is Love and Love is non-judgemental.

Blasphemy, I hear someone cry. Why, then does the word "Christian" mean "Little Christs?" Christ-ness is the greatest potential of us all. Finding Christ-within (or Brahman or whatever your particular belief calls It) is one of our most important missions in life - whatever religion we are. Whether we have a religion or not, what is known as "Christ" is the Divine Identity of *every* human being and we must realize this about ourselves. The Divine Spirit of Love is within everyone, every creature, every thing. Even in the rocks and trees, for there is nowhere where the Holy-Spirit-Mind is not... It's always there, within us all, waiting for us to find It.

We are, at all times, invisibly connected to the JAH-Mind by our spirit-mind, meaning we can access the higher wisdom and abilities of JAH-Mind. Divine Inspiration comes from the connection of mind to Mind. In the Dream-Heaven-Reality, we can control our environment and the very state of our being, for the

48

individual spirit-mind re-unites and becomes one with the universal JAH-Mind and impossibility fades away, for the spirit-mind is God-like and is always within us, meaning that our true Self – our Godness/goodness ("Christ" within) is always present, within ourselves. Hence Psalm 82, verse 6, again, "Ye are gods; and all of you are children of the most High" (see Figure 18, P.109).

In our Dream-Heaven-Reality, the spirit-mind is freed from the restrictions of the body, like when a baby is born, it is freed from the restraint of the womb, so the flesh-death is really a birth back into spirit-mind (our Soulday as opposed to our Birthday). This means freedom from limitation and impossibility, allowing us to become, or do, anything and go anywhere at any given moment. We could become a bird, a vibration, a colour, a sound or music – anything our mind can conceive of, and more.

When our spirit-mind returns to the Dream-Heaven-Reality, our previously restored loved ones will know we are coming and will greet us, having returned to the image of themselves that we will recognize, and they will begin to teach/remind us of what they have learned – our parents are twice our teachers, hence the saying, "Once a man and twice a child." Also, the Bible says, "Suffer little children, and forbid them not to come unto me, for of such is the Kingdom of Heaven," Matthew, Chapter 19, verse 4.

I imagine the people who are restored in the

Dream-Heaven-Reality saying things like, "Wait 'til the kids get here, they're gonna love it," or, "Wait 'til they meet ...." Personally, I look forward to introducing my wife, Bokhabinyana, to my dad, Rick – they are both such wonderful people, I can't imagine how blessed that day will be, she's going to love him as much as he already loves her.

As if to emphasize the validity of this book's message, I noticed, while writing and illustrating it, that the book itself was presenting me with signs which seemed to prove its essential Truth. Look at Figure 17 on P.108, for example, it is a combination of many of the illustrations in the book. See how they all perfectly fit together and form other, hidden images. Even more striking is that the message of "The Comforter", which is summed up in one paragraph on P.77, quite accidentally produced an almost perfectly curved pyramid when I re-arranged the words to try to make the page look more pleasing and the statement more powerful. The book made its own point, as it were!

Chapter 8: Life After Loss

When we learn of someone's restoration, we can either go down into depression, or, in the comfort of the knowledge that **THERE'S NO END TO LIFE, <u>WE CAN LOOK FORWARD TO THE DAY WE SEE THEM AGAIN AND, IN THE MEANTIME, LIVE OUR LIVES TO THE FULL.</u> WE MUST REMIND OURSELVES THAT WHERE THEY ARE NOW, THEY ARE *LITERALLY* STILL ALIVE AND WELL. THEY ARE TRULY FREE. IT IS NEVER TOO LATE TO TALK TO THEM AS THEY CAN HEAR US WHENEVER WE SPEAK TO THEM, SO SPEAK TO THEM, SAY IT OUT LOUD, THEY WILL HEAR YOU. ALSO, DON'T THINK OF THEM BEING IN THEIR COFFIN FOR THEY ARE NOT IN THERE, AS THEY ARE NOT IN THEIR BODY. THIS MEANS THEY CAN BE NEAR US WHEREVER WE ARE, JUST AS WE DON'T HAVE TO GO TO CHURCH OR TEMPLE TO BE NEAR, OR TALK TO THE CREATOR.**

It's strange, but, due to circumstances, I didn't get to spend as much time with my dad as I would have liked, but, since he's been restored, I feel like we spend more time together now, than ever, as he is free from the limitations and obligations of flesh and time and can even be in two places at once – something he would've definitely done in this life if he could.

It is very important that we react to someone's restoration in the right way, using the right language, cultivating the right mind-set, which helps ease the pain of the situation. When I was at my aunt's and my dad's body's funerals, I kept having to repeat to myself that "there is no end to life or love." I just kept saying it to myself over and over whenever I felt down. It really helped me. I suggest you do the same whenever you feel sad, to keep your mind focused on the truth, for the truth shall make us free...free from depression and despair.

Some people react very badly to the news of the restoration of someone close to them, leading to depression, self-neglect, or even self-harm. This is so sad and so unnecessary, as their "lost" loved ones are still with them, hearing their cries and feeling their pain. Rather, we should celebrate their lives and the person they were...*the personality they still are.*

We should remember the good times and the funny moments and laugh. We should talk about them and about how we feel without their *visible* presence, for we should not contain our feelings, as this would have the effect of shaking up a fizzy drink – it will eventually explode. Instead, we should let the pressure out, little by little. Cry if you want. Scream if you want, that is natural and understandable, BUT, always remember they *are* still alive and *you shall* see them again in due time, even if they've been re-incarnated, because the spirit-mind is limitless, so it can be in two or more places at once – even everywhere.

Do whatever you feel you have to do to cope with losing sight of your loved ones, as long as it is not harmful to yourself or others. Celebrate their "Soulday"

– the birth of their spirit-mind into the Dream-Heaven-Reality – and *rejoice in their absolute freedom and complete safety*. Visit the places that hold fond memories of them. Try not to forget to do the things in life which make you happy; the places you like to go, the food you like to eat, the music you like to listen to, the people you like to be around etc... Remember what makes you happy and do it – there's no need to feel guilty about making yourself happy, for if the one you've lost sight of loves you, then *they still want you to be happy...* when you're happy, they're happy.

To see you self-destruct would be so sad for them and your friends and family... and JAH. They all want you to be happy and live your life to the full. Anyone who does not want you to be happy is not worth worrying about, rather pray for them that they, too, find Divine Love within themselves.

This moment in our existence, which we call "our whole life", must be lived in the most positive way possible, so that when we go back to our Source, we can enrich It with the love-energy we have gained. When our spirit-minds return to their Source, freed from association with the flesh, they realize their eternal connection with JAH-Mind; One-ness is realized (yet they do retain their sense of individuality, like the Holy Trinity Itself/Themselves – three "individual" beings with one shared root-identity).

Let nothing spoil your positive attitude. Everything happens for a reason and the reason is always good.

Even when bad things happen, we needn't get so upset or frustrated. Rather we should give thanks for the bad things happening for the hole that negativity creates will be filled and over-flow with positivity. For example, you could have your car stolen, which is a bad thing, but what if you were going to crash in that car and the Creator prevented this from happening by removing the car from your life. Or, say you break your leg and end up saying something to some one at the hospital that changes their life for the better. You could miss your train and be late for your appointment, but end up meeting the man or woman of your dreams on a later train.

This is the positive way we must view life, hence the saying, "Every cloud has a silver lining." Even simple things, like losing your keys, happen for a reason. Once, I went to cross the road but wasn't paying full attention and looked the wrong way first. As I stepped into the road, a car sped passed me and, had I been there a few seconds earlier, it would have run me over. It may have been that earlier that day I couldn't find my keys or I stubbed my toe, delaying my progress to the potential accident. It could have been that I stopped to talk to some one, or heard a song on the radio that I just had to stop and listen to etc... I do not believe that this is just coincidence or luck, as I know it is guidance and protection from the Creator. All is good. Search for the treasure hidden in the mud of every bad situation.

All negative aspects of the physical life are temporary and we don't have to wait until we are no longer in the flesh to be free of them, for we must remember that our mind is created in the likeness of the Mind of JAH; it is creative and a change in mind-set from a negative to a positive outlook is the first step towards healing and taking control over our lives and experiences. This is why the Bible says, "Seek ye first the kingdom of God (JAH-Mind), and his righteousness (God/good thinking and God/good being); and all these things shall be added unto thee."

This means our mind should always be set positively. Even when faced with seemingly hopeless situations, we must try to always trust Love and know that all is guided and all is for good. Trusting in Divine Love is the essence of faith. It's how prayer and meditation work; focusing on the good/God and having faith/knowing that JAH-Love-Mind is real; that It (He/She, They) loves you and will provide you with all you need to be happy and well. We do not really need to ask for anything from JAH-Mind, as It knows, even before we do, what we need and when. We just have to always do what we know is good and right, while keeping faith in JAH Love, giving thanks for life and love. Doing this will mean all will be blessed and positive. Have faith in the the fact that JAH is Love and that Love would only bring good into our lives and would only ever do something drastic if it was absolutely necessary.

Our mind-set is so important to our healing. I was taught that "I can" and "I can't" are both true, *depending on what frame of mind you are in.* For example, if a football player has a clear, easy shot at the goal, he will miss it if he doubts himself; likewise, if he has a long, difficult shot at the goal, he will score if he has faith in his ability. This is because our thoughts can become things. So healing can come from the mind, as disease is really dis-ease; an uneasiness of mind and body. Positivify your mind, positivify your life. Having undesired outcomes in our mind is having faith in the wrong thing; this is the root of fear – the opposite of how we should think, so it's vital we keep our minds positive.

As I said earlier, after my dad's restoration I had several experiences that let me know that he is still alive and well. However, it's now been two years since his body died and I haven't had any of these kind of experiences lately. I think that this is because he's been monitoring my progress since he left my sight and is now confident that I'll be OK, which has allowed his spirit-mind to fully leave the atmosphere of Earth and go forward to his true destiny. I'm sure he still listens to me and keeps checking up on me though; I almost always feel his presence when I'm at work and I sense his continuing pride in me.

So we don't need to think things like, "I wish .... lived to see my kids," or "I wish they could have seen me get married" etc... because they *do* see the things you want them to see. For instance, another friend of mine, Thuli, has also "lost" her father. She told me that some time before his body died, he had been attacked during the years of Apartheid in South Africa and was left blinded. Since his body died, Thuli has had two baby girls, Azania and Ruby. Now, it would be understandable if she wished her dad was still alive to get to know her beautiful girls, BUT, the truth is, he *is* still alive, and because he has been restored in perfection, he is no longer blind and does indeed know *and* see his granddaughters. JAH Bless.

When a partner has been restored, we should not feel guilty if we eventually fall in love with someone new in the future, because, the restored partner's spirit-mind is in a place of Omniscient Mind, meaning that they have full understanding and know that this does not mean you have stopped loving them. Besides, they love you and that means they genuinely want you to be happy and not be lonely. You will *always* love each other and *nothing* will *ever* change that. They know this and so must you.

Therefore, I do not agree with the traditional Christian wedding vow of, "...'til death us do part," because death cannot part us, it only hides one from the others view. A better declaration of true love might be something like, "...to love and to cherish, in flesh and in spirit, forever and ever, as even death cannot part us," because death doesn't stop us from continuing to love each other, for we still love those who have been restored and they still love us and, when we finally re-unite in the Dream-Heaven-Reality, we will all be enveloped in Divine Love, which loves all, equally. There, there can be no jealousy, for Divine Love is different from human love in that it is not just about two people loving each other, it's more like everyone loving everyone as they love themselves, knowing that everyone is part of themselves, and knowing that the very Love they feel is the Spirit of JAH.

Remember, once a person is restored in perfection, their spirit-mind becomes all-understanding, all-forgiving and all-loving as it gradually re-establishes its connection to the Divine Mind. Their mind lives on in a place we have all been before; the Dream-Heaven-Reality of JAH-Mind. It is to this Divine-Mental-Zion (DiMenZion/Dimension) that we shall all return, if we live right, with good intentions and good actions. So live with love. At every opportunity, show love. The more you love, the more eternal-life-love-energy you gain, for truly loving is truly living.

AS YOU READ ON, PLEASE BARE IN MIND THAT I HAVE SURVIVED ALL THE TRAGEDY I SPEAK OF IN THIS BOOK – EVEN THOUGH THERE WERE TIMES I WONDERED IF I COULD – THIS BOOK'S MESSAGE AND THE LOVE AND SUPPORT OF FRIENDS AND FAMILY KEEP ME GOING. I HAVE HEALED SO MUCH... *I'M SURE YOU WILL TOO*, JUST KEEP HOLDING ON TO THE TRUTH!
YOUR SUN *WILL* SHINE AGAIN!

Chapter 9: The Miracle Of LoveLight

This is the 2nd edition of "The Comforter" and this is the new chapter of the book... and indeed my life. This is where my book and message come under some seriously heavy pressure... *from me.* I wrote this book because my wife, Khabi (Bokhabinyana), felt it needed to be shared due to the nature of its message. She made sure it got written and didn't end up like all the other things I know I should do but never end up doing. I originally wrote it in 2009 and now I'm adding this new chapter on 4th July, 2016 and I can't quite believe the ironic twist that follows.

My queen and I had been planning to go to a reggae dance at the seafront, but, just when it was time to go, she decided to stay home, being 8 months pregnant at the time. I begged her to come but she was adamant. So I went to the dance without her, not just for leisure, but also to promote this book. At about 2 in the morning, I got a call – a woman's voice explained that she was a police officer and that she'd got my number from my wife's phone. In that moment, my heart sank, this was not sounding good.

"There's been a fire outside your property and your wife's breathed in a lot of smoke and she's quite poorly." Police came and collected me from the dance to take me to see her at the hospital. I probed the coppers for info about how she was, but they said they knew nothing.

Finally, we reached the hospital and I found myself being ushered through the place in a bit of a daze. Then there she was. Oh God. Oh *NO!* I nearly passed out with shock. She hadn't just breathed in smoke. For two days, the staff did all they possibly could for her, but on the 9th of May, 2016, her body was found to be brain dead. The body of our baby girl had also died. [I will be using capital letters in reference to Them, as I have come to realize that, because Their spirit-minds have now left Their bodies and joined with the Divine-Mind, They, too have taken on/realized Their own Divinity.]

What hurts the most is knowing what kind of person Khabi is; Her Spirit radiated beyond the limits of Her body; one could feel the warmth and brilliance of Her Spirit just from being in Her presence, so anyone who spent any time with Her would know that She embodied pure LoveLight and has a heart of gold. She is the sweetest person you could ever possibly meet. She never got angry with anyone, never held grudges and always went all-out to help others. She is so pure and innocent. She genuinely desired to be the best She can be in the eyes of the Most High. She is not interested in the trappings of this material world, because it has too much negativity, vanity and brutality. She was in this world, but never of it. Sounds familiar, I know, but that's Her... Christ-like! Being chosen by Her felt like I'd been chosen by God-dess Herself! Every moment spent in Her presence was a present. Most mornings I gave thanks for another day together, experiencing life in the presence of Love's Light. I got the best gift God could ever give someone – I GOT TO BE LOVED BY AN *ACTUAL* ANGEL!

So when Her flesh was killed in a deliberate arson attack (the suspect has since pleaded guilty and has been charged with manslaughter, with diminished responsibility), one had to wonder how this could possibly happen... to Her, of all people. How could JAH Love let this happen, when She is such a good person? I mean *nobody* deserves that, but least of all Khabi (what I've noticed about life, though, is that *everyone* suffers in some way or other, it just seems to be the price we pay for this experience in the flesh). Now I find I'm forced to make a decision: Do I believe the Truth I share in this book... or not? Honestly, the answer is I don't believe it... *I know it.*

This whole situation has forced me into a corner. It has made me turn to my own beliefs – my knowledge – and lean all my weight on it. It did not crack. What I know, I know, so I must know it *and live it,* or allow myself to be unnecessarily deceived into the depths of sadness. You see, like the saying, "It's too good to be true" – what has happened to my precious family is *too bad to be true.* It's *so* bad, *so* tragic that I really can't *and don't* believe it – JAH Love would never allow something so unfair to happen... so there *must* be more to life than meets the eye. Khabi was about to prove just how true this is.

At the beginning of the book I spoke about how our first instinct is usually to reject the idea of someone's "death" and I advised you trust your instincts – I still stand by that advice. Right now, this is my advice to me! The truth is that to look at the surface only, focusing

61

solely on what we see before our eyes, is to deceive ourselves, for what we see and experience in this life is not the whole picture, but a fraction of it. That which we *cannot* see with eyes of flesh is the complete, eternal truth. Khabi's story cannot and does not end like this, as this has only happened to the flesh, not the spirit. Whether we live to 1 or 100, our life on Earth is merely a second in our eternal existence, so we must be the best we can be while we're here and make the most positive contributions possible. We must strive to continue to be good and positive, even when faced with such good reasons not to be. The very fact that Khabi and I met on the 9th of May (2008) and Her flesh died on the 9th of May (2016) shows you that there is design to it all; that this was more than just a random act. If Khabi's story was to end just like that, God would have to be sick and twisted. But I know God is Love, so there must be, at some level, a loving reason why this happened.

Khabi's full name, Bokhabinyana, means Radiance in Tswana and was in fact Her granny's mum's name, given to Khabi because Her granny said of Her, "This is my mum!" when She was a baby. Khabi's nature taught me about God. Her poetry – "SPIRIT WORDZ" by Bokhabinyana Radiance LoveLight – is truly inspired: a loud message of truth, empowerment and prophecy said in such a gentle voice. The LoveLight that shines from within Her very Soul matches the beauty one beholds when face to face with Her. Yet, sadly, this beautiful, gentle Soul endured traumatic experiences all Her life. Even when we met She was struggling to survive and throughout our relationship we faced many obstacles together. It really does seem like all the good people suffer the most. Someone compared Khabi's story to that of Jesus – God's only Son, who was innocent and righteous, yet He suffered such a terrible fate. This teaches us that God is ironic. It seems that good people have higher priorities and goals in life and these things are more costly (and longer lasting) than any material acquisition. Because of all the experiences I've had and shared with you in this book, I expected to get some kind of sign from Khabi to prove that She is indeed still alive... what follows is why I *had* to add this chapter to the book.

Around 2009/2010, while we were in Khabi's Motherland, South Africa, I started getting a sharp pain in my chest, like something was lodged in my heart. Sometimes I would feel it just while breathing and had to rub my chest repeatedly to feel better. It affected me the most at night, when I'd find I couldn't spend more than a few minutes laying on my left side before experiencing a sharp pain in my heart area. I would have to turn completely over to feel comfortable again. This remained the case ever since. Six years later, just a couple of days before the fire, Khabi asked me, out of the blue, "Do you still get that pain in your chest?" "Yes" I said. "Don't worry about that," She goes, "I'm gonna heal that for you!" "Yeah," She continued, "that's my next... thing, don't worry about it." Now I did believe She could do something because, previously, I had broken my ribs on my bike and She'd tried to help them heal by placing Her hand very gently on them. To be honest, I didn't feel anything, but when She removed Her hand, it left a perfectly clear and complete hand-print on my skin, so

63

obviously some sort of energy had been present, so I just accepted Her words and thought no more of it. Then, about three days after Her body had died, I woke up in the morning and the first thing I realized was that I was laying on my left side... and there was no pain! I couldn't believe it! That night, I specifically laid down to sleep on my left to see if it would hurt again – NOTHING. Every night since, I have either gone to sleep or woken up on my left – still, no pain. THIS IS NOTHING SHORT OF A MIRACLE! She has kept Her word. From where She is now, She has healed my heart, proving beyond doubt that She is still able to interact with me. My heart bears witness to the miracle of life conquering death. It is a constant, living reminder of the fact that Khabi is still alive, still the Angel-Queen I've always said She is.

I'm still a husband and a dad! Nothing has changed. I will spend the rest of my life looking forward to seeing Her again. I was saying to my good friend Jimmy; "I used to hold Khabi so tight, I'd wrap my arms and legs round Her and squeeeeeze, but it always felt like I couldn't get close enough, as if our bodies were barriers between our souls"... "When my barrier finally drops, *then* we'll be able to get close enough, we'll be one." I patiently wait for that glorious day. Another good friend of mine, Jason, phoned me up and told me that he'd seen the volume of the music on his phone turn down three times in a row. He told me to take time to be still and look out for signs from Khabi. He was right. Many signs followed that are in perfect symmetry with the signs already spoken about in this book.

Since the fire, I've been staying at my mum's flat.

64

One morning we got into the car and we noticed that the interior light was on. It hadn't been on all night otherwise the car battery would have been flat. Plus I remember getting out of the car the night before and it was definitely not on. This parallels what I spoke of in Chapter 3, where the interior light of my Dad's car came on just when we were leaving the cemetery on His birthday. Khabi is well aware of this story and knows we would link the two events together. A sign of life, in the form of light, from LoveLight Herself!

Another night, my mum was watching TV and a programme mentioned how the number 9 represents the end of a cycle. Khabi left the flesh on the 9th of May. Mum then left the room thinking about what this implied and when she returned, the light on the X-Box (that Khabi had bought mum for her birthday) was on. There was no way it could have been accidentally switched on and it hadn't been used for months. It was another sign of life as light, like the lift button lighting up on my Dad's birthday, also mentioned in Chapter 3. The signs continued. One evening, my mum and I were talking about Khabi and my mum suddenly said, "What's that burning smell?" I went to the door, the windows, the other rooms, but I could smell nothing. Mum could still smell it however, so I kept searching. I came close to her and suddenly caught a whiff. I recognised it. It was the smell of paper burning. I knew straight away what this was. When Khabi writes a poem, She burns the edges of the paper with a lighter in the sink, to make it look old. Just as I was explaining this to mum, we both began to smell something else. Again, I recognised the scent. It was our incense. The smell was strong one moment, then completely gone the next. This was confirmation... after singeing Her poetry, Khabi would light incense to take away the smell. SHE IS STILL WRITING HER POETRY!

Time was sweeping by following the fire and the expected due-date of our baby, KaRa, was fast approaching: 20/06/16 – the day after Father's Day. The adverts on TV for Father's Day were getting more frequent and slowly becoming a bit too much to cope with. Then, on 13/06/16, it actually became too much and I found myself getting angrier and sadder by the minute. Then my mum arrived and gave me a newspaper to read. I just paged hastily through it... then my eyes suddenly fixed on a name – "KARA!" I was stunned. Khabi and I had made that name up for our daughter, using the Ancient Egyptian words, "Ka," meaning, "Spirit" and, "Ra," the Divinity of the Sun; "Spirit of the Sun." I've never seen or heard it anywhere before. The story in the paper was about a little girl, Kara, 4, who had been attacked by a large seagull. "Alright KaRa!" I said, "I hear you." I knew my Daughter was sending me a message saying She's OK and I shouldn't be so sad. It really comforted me. Honestly, what were the chances of seeing such a name in the paper? As if that wasn't enough, 4 days later, I was again reading the newspaper and something caught my eye... someone else had been attacked by a seagull. I expected to see some relevance in the story that would make it personal... and there it was. Again, the sign was in the name of the person attacked by the bird; Ian Stewart. My birth-name is Stuart! OK, OK, its spelled differently, I know, but I think

She's a great speller for a pre-birth-aged little girl, don't you? It made me feel so happy and proud – our Daughter's such a clever little girl! [She gets it from Her Mum who's a true genius... I told Her this many times. "Champion Bloodline!" She would say. Please search for and get a copy of Her book of poetry, "SPIRIT WORDZ," the beauty of honesty and enlightenment graces its pages.]

The whole sea-gull thing played on my mind for quite some time. I felt like there was more to it, like there was more to come in connection to sea-gulls. Then one night I was returning to my flat only to find a sea-gull just sitting on the ground next to the gates to my block, apparently unable to fly. I picked it up and took it indoors to save it from the prowling foxes. I thought it would die as it seemed injured, but it survived the night and I took it to the vet the next day. KaRa has been using sea-gulls to communicate with me, so maybe, just maybe, cradling that bird in my arms carried a deeper meaning!?! Nothing would surprise me.

Ever since the fire in May, the weather has been terrible. Leading up to the fire, we'd been lucky and had had several hot, sunny days – it was shaping up to be a good summer – but since this tragedy happened, there has been nothing but cold, rainy, gloomy days. A whole months worth of rain fell in one day. Some weeks later, things got
worse; a months worth of rain fell in a single night! This caused floods and chaos. It was as if the heavens were crying with me. It's July, it should be summer. Khabi's

flesh-murder is a catastrophe for the whole of mankind, because Her Radiance brought a Light brighter than the sun into this world; Her words, Her actions, Her intentions, Her poetry and Her presence were a beacon of hope and an example of righteousness that, without any effort at all, raised peoples potential and ability from the depths to the heights. She is the purest person I've ever met – I never knew a human being could be so pure and innocent, so it is no surprise to see this kind of response from the planet. The heavens continued to weep.

I had been back to the flat once to clean it with my friends, Jason, Anne and Solomon, who had come all the way from London to help me because every surface in every room was covered in greasy black soot. Eventually, I got the urge to go back to the flat and clean it a bit more
with mum. The day was chilly and gloomy and it had been raining heavily in the morning. However, the moment we stepped into the front room in front of the window, the sun suddenly came out and filled the whole room with brilliant sunshine. It was as though the sun had never shone before and was making an extra Radiant show. We were just amazed by it – rain and gloom all month, then bam! Pure sunshine, here, now! That very day... was KaRa's expected Earthday. *KaRa! – Spirit of the Sun!* Hence the sun-sign we were greeted with. Our Daughter is forever the Spirit of the Sun because She never entered the corruptible body of limitation; She is quite literally an eternally free Spirit – a free Ka: Afreeka/Africa!

In the last days of Khabi's "journey through time," as She calls this life in Her poetry, She kept saying how She kept noticing the clock saying 11:11, which She said She'd read was an auspicious moment in time. She commented on it many times and I told Her that it reminded me of how I used to like seeing the time 7:47, when I was a kid, because it reminded me of my Dad, who used to fly on 747 aeroplanes. Then, some time after Khabi had been restored, I woke up and thought to myself, "Check the time," It was 7:47. You know I don't believe in mere coincidence. You know by now that everything has a reason, no matter how seemingly insignificant it may be. For me, this was cause for a smile :-) I went back to sleep and had a bit of a lay-in (which was well needed at the time). Then I got up, got showered and dressed and when I returned to the bedroom, I looked at the clock – it was 11:11! This made me pay more attention to the clock. That night I woke up in the early hours and turned round to check the clock – 3:47 – nothing special about that. So I thought to myself, "What would be a significant time to see? Ah! 9:05" (our anniversary, 09/05) and went back to sleep. When I woke up, I scrambled to see the clock... 9:05! She's *still* waking me up! Lol! This was very comforting to me as I was still really struggling with what had happened.

The next morning, I woke up, checked the clock... 9:05 *again!* Later that morning I was sitting, staring out into the garden at mum's flat, when I saw a plume of smoke rise up from near a chair in the garden. I assumed it was mum out there, smoking, but I soon realised that she was in the bathroom. I watched the cloud rise up into the trees, where it lingered and weaved among the branches and leaves. I really wondered what it was. No one else was there. I went out to it and began sniffing the air to try to identify it. I wondered if next door was having a barbecue... but there was no smell. I went back indoors and sat and watched it. It was still there in the tree!?! Then, like a wave of mist, it slowly drifted towards the top of the open back door, where, like a rippling blanket, it sloped downwards and filled the doorway. I walked up to it and sniffed the air, but still nothing. The mist disappeared but as I moved I could see something was still there glinting in the early morning sun. I knew who was visiting me! Khabi loves trees and often hugs them, soaking up their love energy. Nothing has changed, which is why the mist paid so much attention to the tree first! This was not the last of this mist-tree mystery. A good friend of ours, Sister Karin, had flown from Cape Town to the UK for Khabi's body's funeral and stayed at mum's flat (I moved back to my flat, although it was – and still is – covered in soot. Not the nicest experience). She explained to us that one night, she had been getting ready to go to sleep, when she felt a heat on her back. Then she heard a familiar call from behind her. She turned around and *actually saw* Khabi in full-living colour, but, she said, "It was like She was in a mist!" Wow! What a confirmation of Khabi's Soul's survival!

Since Khabi was restored, I had only dreamt of Her once and it was very, very brief – I saw Her face and She was smiling and Her face was not burnt. Better still, She was almost glowing, Her face had a golden brilliance to it

– a Radiance. I was so pleased to see She was OK, but I wanted more... I needed more and I kept wondering why I wasn't having any dreams about Her. Then, exactly 2 months after the fire – at almost exactly the same time as the fire was started, I finished updating Khabi's poetry book, "SPIRIT WORDZ" (sorry I keep ruthlessly plugging Her book, I'M JUST SO EXTREMELY PROUD OF HER AND HER MESSAGE, which I believe is of great importance to all humanity – MISSION ACCOMPLISHED, WELL DONE BABY!!!).

The following morning, I woke up and, instead of getting up I thought, "Nope, I need a lay-in" and went back to sleep. This was the dream-vision that followed: I woke up hot and unable to breathe properly. I pushed the bed covers off and made my way to the window, but I was still struggling to breathe. Then Khabi joined me by the window! As I leaned out the window to get a proper breath of fresh air I nearly knocked one of my ornaments out the window – it was all so real. Then Khabi said She was going to bathe. I turned and watched Her as She walked off and I noticed a small burn on Her back. Then it all came flooding back; the fire!.. but here She is! I stared at Her face again. I was *so* happy. *"You're back!"* I exclaimed. "Yeah!" She said. "But you died in the fire!" I continued, "And now you're back!" "Yeah, I know!" She said with a beaming smile. I just grabbed Her and held Her in my arms. I cried with such joy that I could hardly get my words out, but as I held Her, my prayer was simply this; "Father-Mother-God, thank You *so* much for bringing my Queen back to me!" She went all shy and bashful, as She always did, and that was the image I was

71

left with as I woke up. I'm *so* glad I listened to that "inner–JAH–Voice" and got the chance to have that vision.

I must tell you, lastly, that there was a Rastafari elder that Khabi and I used to know, called Red–I, who was always such a blessing to meet and greet in the street. Sadly, His body was suffering from lung cancer and eventually died. On our way to His memorial dance, we noticed that the moon was red. Yes I! A red moon for Red–I! Recently I was speaking with His daughter, Rachel I–Kaya and was explaining that there is no death; that her dad is still alive, just hidden by a veil. She agreed and told me she had actually seen her dad since His flesh died. In fact, she revealed to me that the time she saw Him, He was standing next to me... at the reggae dance... the night of the fire! So many signs and many more have happened since! What more do we need? Khabi and KaRa are definitely alive and very well and They are waiting patiently for me to join them in the Eternal Love–Light–Life in the Dream–Heaven–Reality, in JAH–Mind. I will spend the rest of my days knowing They are with me always, like the Holy Spirit – OMnipresent. So I guess my prayers for a miracle *have* been answered, for in truth Khabi and KaRa have survived death and gone Home. Wherever they go, I will always follow, so one special day, I know I'll be coming Home to my beautiful eternal family.

In this book, I have given you all that I know to be true. This truth is the very thing keeping me sane at this precise moment in time. Honestly, if I forget the truth, even for a moment, I just feel myself sinking and can cry 'til I can't catch my breath and nearly pass out. The only thing that brings me back from that point is remembering that *God really wouldn't do something like this;* that <u>in the true Spirit-Life, THIS HASN'T ACTUALLY HAPPENED</u>; death *really is* an illusion of the flesh, only *seeming* real from the *body's* perspective... the body, which itself, was never the living personality we knew them by; It was the body-dwelling spirit-mind that we knew and loved that gave the body life, for the true identity of one's body is not *itself*, but its *self; one's Self... One!* Remember...

every*BODY* dies, *yet*, every*ONE* lives forever.
* THE SUN NEVER REALLY SETS! *

A Lasting Vision

I just want to finish off by sharing one last thing with you. I *have* to tell you about this dream-vision I had of Khabi – there's no way I could end this book without it.

The vision began with me finding myself getting off the bus, in town, opposite Southend Victoria station. Now, everything about the scenery was perfectly accurate and it was a particularly beautiful day – the sun was shining and lighting up the leaves, giving the trees an almost translucent spring-green/yellowish glow, while the breeze made the trees twinkle with life. Oh Nature!

I admired all this in the few moments I spent before turning round to find Khabi getting off the bus with me! *Oh gosh,* you can imagine how pleased I was to see Her! I was greeting Her as though She'd risen from the grave! I just threw my arms round Her. Pulling my head back to look at Her, I just stared at Her beaming face! Pure Radiance! Sunshine!

In that moment, it all came flooding back – *the happiness!* For the first time in a long time I was feeling and remembering how *great* it felt being with Her! *Now, that's not something one can imagine!* You have to *be* there, basking in Her Radiance to know what it's like! It's a bit like sun-bathing in an unimaginably beautiful place, where Love, Herself, is the Heavenly Body bathing you in warm inner peace – an almost *religious* experience!

I know I wasn't just dreaming all this up because during the vision, I specifically took an inner moment to consciously check that what I was seeing and experiencing was indeed real. I took a breath in to make sure I was breathing – I was. I quickly glanced about at my surroundings – nothing was amiss and I was fully aware of my senses and thoughts. I also noticed we were both wearing black.

I couldn't stop smiling, looking deep into Her dazzling eyes as we walked. I could even feel the awkward jolting of our steps as we struggled along, still clinging to each other. As we crossed the road the tears began to run. I looked up with blurry eyes to see that a woman in a car waiting at the lights saw me cry as our eyes met and, for a split second, I felt embarrassed. I'm telling you, THIS WAS REAL! Having crossed the road, we turned to face each other to properly cuddle.

We just stood there, holding tight! I could actually *feel* Her in my arms! Emotionally, and muffled in Her neck and shoulder, I said, "Oh Babe! How am I gonna remember this forever!?!" What I meant was *"I have to remember this forever!"* Then I woke up... HAPPY! I can honestly say, hand on heart, that *reunion with our "lost" loved ones awaits us all* in the LoveLight of the Dream-Heaven-Reality. Trust me... *I KNOW... 'COS I'VE ALREADY TASTED THAT JOY!*

THE
COMFORTER:

is
that
the truth
sets us free,
so let the truth
of life's eternalness
give us relief from grief,
for our lives last for eternity,
while this physical life is fleeting
and precious so we shouldn't let anyone
or anything prevent us from living life happily.

...&...

the
Source
and
Destination
of all life
is JAH-Mind;
Divine Love-Mind.
Life is Love;
Love is Eternal-Life-Love-Energy
(see the heart on the cover of the book);
our spirit-mind is connected to JAH-Mind
which is Eternal Life Itself;
Eternal Love Herself;
Divine-Love-Light.
Have no fear,
have no sorrow,
there truly is
an eternal tomorrow.
Celebrate life's eternalness.
To
one and all,
love and happiness,
always.
Bless.

Words Of Wise Mind

Mary Elizabeth Frye:
"Do not stand by my grave and cry, I am not there, I did not die."
- From the poem, "Do Not Stand By My Grave And Weep (I Am Not There, I Do Not Sleep)."

John Donne:
"...Those, whom thou (death) think'st thou dost overthrow, die not, poore death, nor yet can'st thou kill me.
- From the poem, "Death Be Not Proud."

H.I.M. Emperor Haile Selassie I:
"Death...Who is this woman? Take her away from me."

"We are confident in the victory of good over evil."

Joseph Hill:
"Life is like a mirror, reflect on what you do, and if your face is smiling, it will smile right back to you."
- From the song, "Behold."

Albert Einstein:
"Science without religion is lame. Religion without science is blind."

"When the answers come easily, it's God talking."

Robert Nesta Marley OM:
"Why do you look so sad, and forsaken? Don't you know,

when one door is closed, another is open."
  – From the song, "Coming In From The Cold."

"My music fights against the system that teaches to live and die."

"Let us chase away the devils with a thing named love."

"Forget your sorrows and dance, forget your troubles and dance, forget your sickness and dance, forget your weakness and dance."
  – From the song, "Them Belly Full, But We Hungry."

"Emancipate yourself from mental slavery, none but ourselves can free our minds"
  – From the song, "Redemption Song."

"While I'm gone, every thing's gonna be alright"... "Oh my little sister, don't shed no tears, no, no woman, no, woman no cry."
  – From the song, "No Woman No Cry."

Damian & Stephen Marley:
"And it was written up in the book of life that a man shall endure for evermore"... "Did you know destruction of the flesh is not the ending to life"... "Did you know that I exist before the Earth"... "The body's just a vehicle, transporting the soul, it's what's inside of people is beauty to behold."
  – From the song, "It Was Written."

Arrested Development:
"Space ain't man's final frontier. Man's final frontier is the soul, guided by someone more powerful than any human being; someone felt, but never seen; you will be surprised
of what resides in your insides."
- From the intro, "Man's Final Frontier."

Michael Joseph Jackson:
"Planet Earth...are you just a speck of dust, in a mindless void...something tells me this isn't true."

Kymani Marley:
"So much things I'd like to know and so much things to say, but I'm gawn save it, 'cos I know we'll be together some day."
- From the song, "Dear Dad."

Capelton:
"Fear is in the eyes of the beholder and love is in the presence of the love-maker, <u>life is in the words of The Comforter</u>, endure much longer, live much longer."
- From the song, "It Was Written."

Beres Hammond:
"Oh Sun, it's gonna shine again, 9 out of 10, it's gonna shine again."
- From the song, "Gonna Shine Again."

Zahara:
"Some day your broken heart will mend, yeah, and you will find your smile again, yeah, yeah, so take your time

for time is what it's gonna take and then, you awake to
find there's one less tear. I believe your healed. You'll
heal, you will."
 – From the song, "My Guitar."

Bokhabinyana Radiance LoveLight:

"We forgot that in our culture, death only ever meant
rebirth, a transformation into higher dimensions."
 – From the poem, "& Then Fear Happened To
   Make Us Forget."

"I rise from the ashes, Empowered & wholly restored,
Healed & complete, Unsinged like Shadrach, Meschach &
Abednego"... "Free to bask in the purity of unspeakable
bliss"... "I have passed through the door of TRUTH"... "I
pre-exist time, One with the entire cosmos & beyond"...
"Radiant like the beaming sunrise, I rise to greet the
dawning of infinite LOVE & infinite LIGHT, The Beauty
of Eternal Day."
 – From the poem, "Rising Phoenix."

Figure 1: Mary, Mary, Not Contrary

This is an image of the Ancient Egyptian Goddess, Isis, nursing her child, Horus. The similarities between this image and those of Mary with Jesus are quite apparent. The Holy child even raises his finger as does Jesus in many paintings. This does not mean, however, that because the Egyptian version is older, the Christian Mary is just a copy, it is a remnant of ancient Truth. Neither does the fact that Mary and Jesus are Christian figures mean that the Egyptian version is to be deemed unrighteous pagan idolatry, as it is the original ancient Truth, itself. They are not contrary to one another. They are revelations of the same truth in different places at different times.

Figure 2: AUM's The Word

    This is the symbol of the sound AUM, the creative vibration that Hindus believe brought everything into existence. It is the Hindu equivalent of "the Word" that the Bible says was instrumental in the Creation of the universe. This Aum is also Amen in the Bible, Amin in Islam, Amun in Ancient Egyptian religion, etc... which, again, shows that Truth is universal. AUM can also be equated to the sound of "the big bang", the sound of Creation. Sound always accompanies creation, just as when we were born, sound announces Creation. The sound of Creation, AUM, is musical, hence we call the Cosmos the Uni-Verse, The One Song. All is Divine Music. Music is life.

Figure 3: He's Got The Whole World... In His Head

This is a picture I painted to show how everything was created from thought in JAH-Mind. The first image shows God thinking to Himself, meditating. The second image equates creating light with the idea of Creation, because the Bible says that God created light at the beginning of Creation and in most cartoon strips, when someone has an idea, it is represented as a light bulb appearing above their head; the light is a flash of inspiration; light caused by thought. The next image shows the "big bang" happening. The big bang theory is used to discredit the existence of a Creator, but here I'm saying the big bang was caused by the Creator. Then we see the universe appearing after the big bang. My intention is to show how God the Father (Divine Masculine) used His Mind – the Holy Spirit (Divine Feminine) – to bring everything into existence. In the beginning was the Word, but before the Word there had to have been the Thought. This means that in the very beginning, all that ever existed was the Eternal Divine Mind, the Holy Spirit, which thought-brought God and the universe into being.

Figure 4: Divine Figure

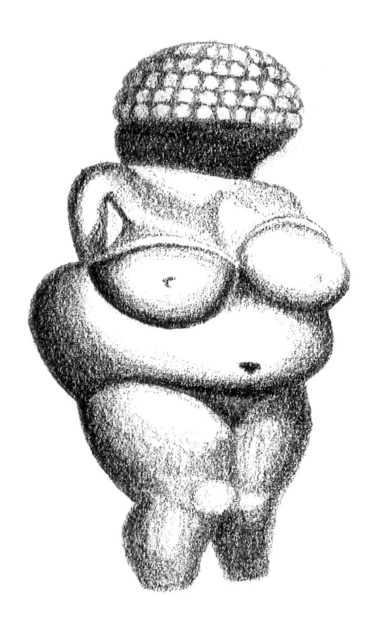

This is the "Venus of Willendorf," a tiny carving named after where it was found in Austria. She was carved around 30,000 years ago. Many similar figurines have been found all around the world and are generally believed to be fertility dolls or Mother Goddess figurines. My theory is that they actually represent the Holy Spiritess; the Source of everything... *including God.* Venus is the name generally given to most ancient depictions of the Sacred Feminine, but other names include Isis, Kali, Aphrodite, Sophia and Mary. Her figure, her shape, is Divine in that it represents the miraculous life-causing, life-bearing and life-sustaining attributes of the Divine Feminine – and women in general – in abundance, emphasizing Her natural creative ability and power. This beautiful, unmistakably African woman (see, "Ancient Future" by Wayne B Chandler, essential knowledge, thank you sir) is, therefore, possibly the best way to depict the Creator; the pre-God Goddess, the First Cause – *the Creatoress of All.*

Figure 5: Life Is Love And Light

Here we can see the similarity between the Egyptian symbol for "life," the Ankh, at left, the symbol for Venus, the planet of love, at centre, which also the symbol of Femininity, or the Divine Feminine, or Wisdom/Enlightenment/"light," at right. The Ankh means Life because it actually represents the Divine Feminine, Omega, in unity with the Divine Masculine, Alpha. It is the unification of Father God and Mother Goddess, from which all life and material comes. So I believe these symbols and the "Venus" figurines, like the one in Figure 4, all represent the same thing – the original creative force, which is Love.

Figure 6: Hand Signed

ALLA

When one puts one's hands together as above, the life lines, heart lines and head lines spell out the name "Alla," again proving that the One God is communal to all people of any religion and non-believers. No one religion is true and the others false as *all religions and people have the same God in common.*

Figure 7: The Universe In A Nutshell... In The Nut

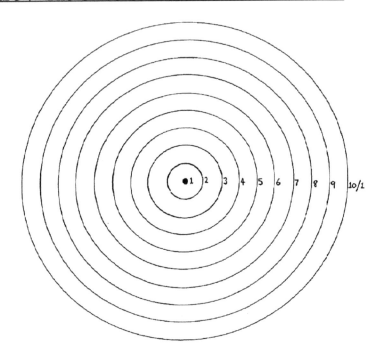

Key:
1 – JAH–Mind/Holy Spirit
2 – Human Spirit
3 – Human Mind
4 – Atoms Of Our Body
5 – Body
6 – Earth/World
7 – Solar System
8 – Universe
9 – Dream–Heaven–Reality
10 – JAH–Mind/Holy Spirit

1 to 5 = JAH Within Us
5 to 10 = Us Within JAH

Explanation

This is my diagram of the Universe. In verse 77 of the Gospel of Thomas, Jesus says to His Disciples, "Split a piece of wood: I am there." Plainly speaking, this refers to God's Omnipresence, but, I knew there was a deeper level to this. I meditated on this for a while (for days), then thought of the concentric circles within a tree. This was when I realized that these circles represented God and the Universe as I have described here. The same verse goes on to say, "He who shall find the interpretation of these words shall not taste of death."

1 is the same as 10, in that $1+0=1$ and, in this diagram, you can see how 1, the beginning, is the same as 10, the end and vice-versa. This is the eternal nature of the Universe. The outside is the inside and the inside is outside. God is the biggest Thing in the Universe, as It surrounds All, while, at the same time, God is the *smallest* Thing in the Universe, as It is within our very atoms. This is what is meant when the Bible says that God is the Alpha and the Omega, for He/She/They/It is the beginning and end of all things; an eternal cycle of end meeting beginning, over and over; a circle, whose end is its beginning, hence, "World without end." We come from a non-physical, mental state and enter the flesh. Then we leave the flesh and return to our original mental state, meaning that our origin is our destination. The diagram places us in the 5th circle – the body, that is within JAH-Mind (10) and, simultaneously, has JAH-Mind within itself (1), showing how the Holy Spirit can be within everything, while at the same time, surround

everything: Omnipresence. It also explains its Omniscience, for everything is in its Mind and Its Mind is in everything. This means it is impossible to be apart from the Creator. We are never lost, so when we search for God, we should look inwards. JAH-Mind is within our very atoms; the Divine Intelligence that tells our cells what to do when we need to heal, fight infection or grow.

Atoms are spheres that rotate in circles. Planets do the same. Planets are the atoms of the Body of the Universe, molecules of thought within JAH-Mind. Points 4 to 8 represent our physical reality. Points 9 to 3 are the unseen, spiritual-mental reality. Point 9, Dream-Heaven-Reality, is what lies beyond the material Universe; it is the end of materiality and the beginning of Mentality. This means that if you got into a rocket and flew in a straight line, your rocket and physical self would eventually come to the edge of the physical universe; the limit of physical existence, beyond which all that exists is in the Mental realm of the Creator's Mind... which is within you. The outside is the inside and vice-versa, so if you go on an inward journey into your body, into your atoms and beyond, you will eventually find a Universe and JAH again – that which surrounds all is within all. Outside the Universe you would find JAH-Mind – point 10, while within one's self you would find point 1: JAH-Mind, again, so, in a nutshell, JAH-Mind is like a nut within nine shells, with the ninth shell simultaneously being the nut within. JAH-Mind envelopes the Universe, while at the same time, it is within the very atoms of everything, everywhere.

Figure 8: Back To Life

MIND = LIFE

And

MIND + BODY = LIFE

But

BODY – MIND = DEATH

So

BODY = DEATH

Yet

LIFE – BODY = MIND

And

MIND = LIFE

Explanation

Before we were born, we were a spirit in our mind. Our mind was at one with the Mind of the Creator. We have always been alive. When we were born into this physical life, our living spirit-mind was merely delivered into a body. The body itself does not have life, hence, when we are unconscious, the body is not responsive [The word "unconscious" is another misleading term, as only the body is affected, not the mind, as people have experienced visions and awareness whilst being "unconscious"]. Our already living spirit-mind becomes en-bodied in new flesh simply to be able to experience the physical world, so our *birth*day is really just our *Earth*day; the beginning of our flesh-life, but not the beginning of our actual life and it may not even be our first or last visit to Earth. We live our Earth-bound life and then the spirit-mind returns back to its Source, leaving the dead body behind. The flesh-death is simply the re-release of the spirit-mind into eternal freedom and love.

Life truly is a circle. **FROM THE PERSPECTIVE OF THE SPIRIT-MIND, THERE IS NO END TO, OR BREAK IN LIFE, JUST A RETURN TO A HIGHER, FREER LEVEL OF CONSCIOUSNESS; CONTINUOUS CONSCIOUSNESS; AN ETERNAL, UN-INTERRUPTED LIFE. DEATH ONLY EXISTS FROM THE BODY'S PERSPECTIVE, WHILE THE PERSON(ALITY) WE KNOW AND LOVE LIVES ON OUTSIDE THE BODY. WE COME FROM MIND AND RETURN TO MIND, HAVING USED OUR BODY FOR THE GAINING OF KNOWLEDGE AND, MOST IMPORTANTLY, TO GAIN AND SHARE LOVE, FOR <u>LOVE IS THE ENERGY OF ETERNAL LIFE. OUR WHOLE REASON FOR BEING IS TO EXPERIENCE AND EXPRESS LOVE. THIS IS THE MEANING OF LIFE.</u>** <u>JAH is pure , original, Divine Love and what would be the point of having love when there is no one to experience and enjoy it? This is the main reason we were created in the first place.</u>

Figure 9: Drink Of Life

A simplification (I hope) of Figure 8:

WATER = A DRINK

And

WATER + A GLASS = A DRINK

But

A DRINK – WATER = A GLASS

And

A GLASS = NO DRINK

Yet

A DRINK – A GLASS = WATER

And

WATER = A DRINK

(See explanation overleaf)

Explanation

Water does not need a glass to be a drink, just as our spirit-mind does not need a body to be alive. The water existed before the glass. The glass was never part of the water, it merely contained it, to aid its utilization. If the glass breaks, the water does not break with it, but, instead, it runs free, like it was before being confined in the glass.

Furthermore, the water can not be destroyed – if you freeze it, it becomes ice, if you boil it, it becomes vapour, which becomes one with the atmosphere, if you separate its elements, it becomes hydrogen and oxygen and if you drink it becomes part of you. In fact no thing can be utterly destroyed – if you burn paper, it becomes heat and light and smoke which become one with the atmosphere. If you crush a brick, it becomes dust, if you burn wood, you get charcoal, etc, etc...

Figure 10: Five Births And A Funeral

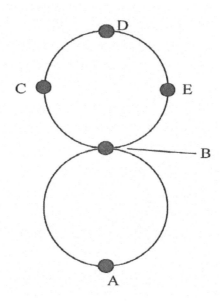

Key:

A – JAH Life
B – Dream-Heaven-Reality
C – Flesh-Birth
D – Flesh-Life
E – Flesh-Death

A – JAH-Life

    This, the root Source of our existence, is where our spirit-minds dwell at one with JAH-Mind. Here we experience our first birth, being born from A, the Unity of JAH-Mind, into individuality as a separate spirit-mind in B, although we still remain mentally connected to JAH-Mind.

B - Dream-Heaven-Reality

This is where we exist between being a spirit in JAH-Mind and being a spirit in a body on Earth. It is also where we can access the realm of the physical universe while in spirit form. Here is where our spirit-minds are born into a body, our second birth. The spirit-mind can enter and exit its new body at will, but returns permanently once the body starts to breathe its own air, hence the Bible says in Genesis, Chapter 2, verse 7, that when God breathed life into the nostrils of man, he became a living soul.

This would mean that when a stillbirth, abortion or miscarriage happens, the spirit-mind of the baby simply doesn't get to remain in the baby's body, but survives nonetheless; the spirit-mind of the baby remains in the place it probably spent most of its time whilst awaiting the birth of its body... present in the world, yet invisible, all around the mother and father, rather than being confined within the mother, fully able to hear, feel *and* *see* its parents. This is why babies sometimes look at us so deeply – they recognize us, not just by voice alone.

Life is eternal for all, even the un-bodily-born. This is why the spirits of miscarried, stillborn and aborted babies have been detected around the family by psychics and even appear in some photos. These babies never experience the death of the flesh the way we do, as their spirit-mind would undoubtedly *not* have been present in the body when it died.

C - Flesh-Birth

This is when our bodies are born into this world from the womb. Our birthday is just the beginning of our body's life - our Earthday. It's actually our spirit's third birth.

D - Flesh-Life

This is where we are now; a combination of spirit and flesh living in the material world.

E - Flesh-Death

This is actually our fourth birth, where we are born back into the non-physical Dream-Heaven-Reality at point B, where we decide whether our fifth birth should be a progression into point A, back into JAH-Mind, or to go back and be re-born into flesh at point C.

The diagram, which resembles the symbol of infinity , ∞, shows that when we live the ideal, righteous life of love, we go from point A, anti-clockwise to point B, then clockwise from B to B again and then returning, anti-clockwise, to point A. In one life, from A, B, C, D, E, B to A, we actually experience five births and no death, as the funeral is for the body alone, not for the spirit-self.

Figure 11: What Mind's More, Matter's Not

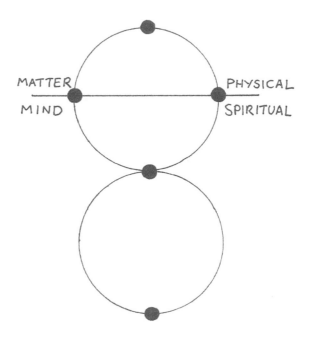

Here we can see that we spend more of our existence in mind than in matter, meaning that the state of mind matters more than the state of our flesh, for our mind is our true self, while our body is just our matter. Mind affects matter, so mind matters most. It's hard to remain healthy when your thoughts are not.

Figure 12: The Re-Incarnation Loop

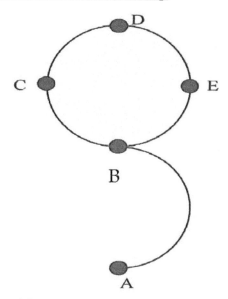

In figure 10, we saw how the ideal route of one life goes through points A, B, C, D, E, B and A. Here, though, we see that if re-incarnation occurs, we enter into a loop, in a cycle of birth, death, birth, death, instead of returning to our Source, so the spirit-mind does not progress from point E to B and back to A, but will instead go from E to B and return to flesh at point C, where it begins to loop (C, D, B, E/ C, D, B, E, etc...), until it finally fulfils its purpose and returns to A, where it can remain for eternity or until it wishes (or is required) to return to Earth again. Between physical lives, the reincarnating spirit-mind will indeed witness the glory of the Dream-Heaven-Reality, if only briefly. However, there is no such thing as time in that dimension of Love's Light, so they will still be there to greet you when you get there.

Figure 13: What Comes Down, Must Go Up

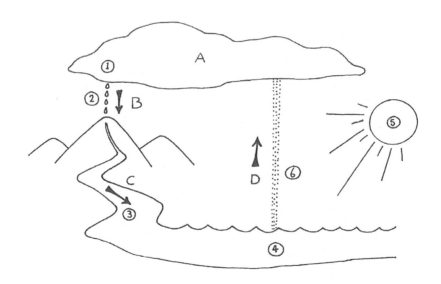

Key:

The Water Cycle	The Life Cycle
1 – Cloud	1 – JAH–Mind
2 – Raindrop	2 – Sprit–Mind
3 – Stream	3 – Baby
4 – Sea	4 – Adult
5 – Sun	5 – "The Light"
6 – Evaporation	6 – Restoration

Explanation

The Water Cycle	The Life Cycle
A – A raindrop is part of the cloud.	A – A spirit-mind is part of JAH-Mind.
B – The raindrop separates and falls to Earth.	B – The spirit-mind separates and falls to Earth.
C – The raindrop enters a stream, a small body of water, which flows into a larger body of water, the sea.	C – The spirit-mind enters a baby, a small body of a human, which grows into a larger body of a human, an adult.
D – Being in the sun, vapour evaporates from the sea, rising up to returns to its original state in a cloud.	D – Seeing "the light", the spirit-mind separates from the body, rising up to return to its original state in JAH-Mind.

Figure 14: Three Lives In One

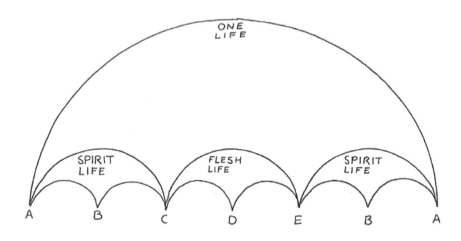

This diagram is an expansion of figure 10. If we lay points A to A of Figure 10 out in a line, we can see more clearly how we go from spirit to flesh and back to spirit again; three separate stages of one life, with A, B and C being the very same spirit-life as found in E, B and A. [Figure 15, P.105 develops this diagram into a symbol of the three stages of one, continuous life.]

Figure 15: Three Lives In One, Too

A continuation of Figure 14, where I have added the ankhs to clearly define the three stages of one life, which will become the basis of further images on this theme.

Figure 16: Sharing Spirit

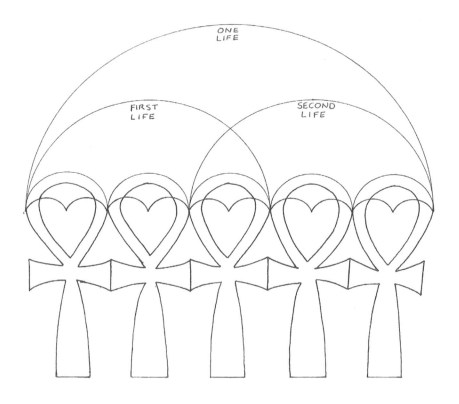

Explanation

This Figure shows what happens when we are reincarnated from one body to the next; how the spirit-life after restoration is actually the very same spirit-life we have before and after each physical life. The spirit-life in the middle is where our previous physical life over-laps the next physical life in the Dream-Heaven-Reality and any amount of time can pass here – forwards *or* backwards in time. This is where we are in the world, but body-less, where spirit-minds can become seemingly trapped and can manifest as ghosts. [Ghosts are real, but on the whole, they are harmless, as ghosts are people and only some people are badly behaved. Ghosts are simply the spirit-minds of people who are so entrenched in the idea of there only being a physical world that they find it hard to leave it behind and progress along the proper path of their continuing journey. This is why it is so important to cultivate a spiritual mentality, to realize that there is much more to life than life on Earth.] More importantly, this is where we can commune between the spirit and material worlds; the meeting of minds.

Figure 17: All In One

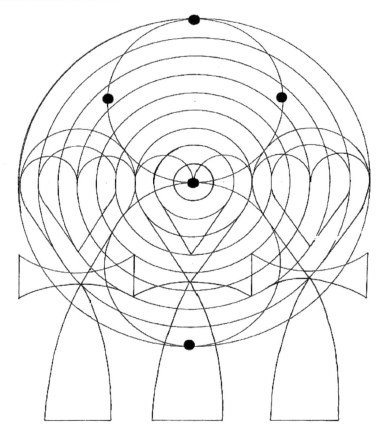

This figure combines most of the previous diagrams into one symbol, comprised of love, life, birth, restoration, Unity, Trinity, the Universe, spirit, matter and eternity. To my surprise, when I completed this diagram, I noticed that it contained many hidden symbols within it, suggesting to me that my message is correct on many levels. Can you see them? Do you see the dove? Study this image, colour it in if you wish, and find more symbols and meaning; let it give you your own interpretation of it. Amongst other things, it made me think of the image on P.16.

This image is meant to represent the location of the Kingdom of Heaven within us – in our mind, right between our eyes, where the third eye or pineal gland is located. When one travels within one's self, one finds one's God–Self. You begin with **y**ou and end up at **Y**ou. Why do you think we write the "i" that refers to one's self as a capital? Are we seeing i to I?

Figure 19: Beginning At The End

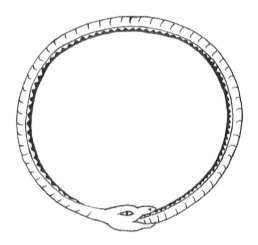

This image is called Ouroboros, which shows end meeting beginning. Alpha is the beginning and Omega is the end, but when the two become one, there is no end, just continual life. Hence the ankh, symbol of life, is made of the symbols for Alpha and Omega (see next figure). Life has no beginning or end, we just eternally exist in a variety of forms and realities.

Figure 20: 1 + 1 = 3

Here we see the representation of God's miracle –
Eternal Life, caused by Love, when Divine Masculine
combines with Divine Feminine, when One eternal life
joins with the other One, They make a Third eternal life;
Alpha + Omega = Eternity.

The 12 Keys

Here are, listed together, the 12 passages that convey the over-all message of "The Comforter," which have been highlighted in bold capitals throughout the book. The page numbers in brackets refer to their original place in the text.

1

I HAVE CALLED THIS BOOK, "THE COMFORTER," AS I BRING YOU GOOD NEWS; THAT ETERNAL LIFE IS AUTOMATIC AND IS FOR EVERYONE. IN THIS BOOK, I WILL SHARE WITH YOU MY OWN PERSONAL EXPERIENCES AND REVELATIONS ABOUT LIFE WHICH HAVE HELPED MY FRIENDS, FAMILY, STRANGERS AND MYSELF DURING THE DIFFICULT TIMES OF LOSS – MY HOPE IS THAT THEY HELP YOU TOO. (P.1)

2

THE DICTIONARY'S DEFINITION OF DEATH: "DYING, END OF LIFE; END" – GIVES THE IMPRESSION THAT WHEN OUR BODIES DIE, IT'S ALL OVER, FINISHED. THIS MISCONCEPTION CONTRIBUTES TO OUR SORROW, WHILE GOING AGAINST THE TEACHINGS OF NEARLY <u>EVERY</u> RELIGION OR SPIRITUAL BELIEF SYSTEM IN THE WORLD, BOTH PAST AND PRESENT. (P.3)

3

I DO NOT SAY, "REST IN PEACE" AS WHEN THEY ARE FREE FROM THE FLESH, THEY HAVE NO NEED TO

REST, IN FACT THEY BECOME INVIGORATED WITH THE LIMITLESS ENERGY OF LIFE, NO LONGER RESTRICTED BY THE FLAWS OF THE FLESH, SUCH AS FATIGUE, DISEASE, DISABILITY OR OLD AGE. NEITHER DO I SAY THINGS LIKE "I LOVE_D_ THEM SO MUCH," BECAUSE THEY ARE _STILL_ ALIVE AND I _STILL_ LOVE THEM, JUST AS THEY STILL LOVE ME. (P.4)

4

THE PEOPLE WHO LEAVE THE FLESH REMAIN AMONGST US FOR SOME TIME AND CAN COME AND GO, CHECKING UP ON US FROM TIME TO TIME. THIS IS WHY IT IS IMPORTANT NOT TO LET GRIEF PREVENT US FROM LIVING A NORMAL LIFE, FOR THEY SEE US, HEAR US AND FEEL US; THEY STILL LOVE US AND WANT US TO BE HAPPY. (P.15)

5

LIFE IS THE ENERGY OF THE SPIRIT, WHICH IS LOVE. SCIENCE TEACHES US THAT ENERGY CANNOT BE CREATED OR DESTROYED, IT CAN ONLY CHANGE FROM ONE STATE TO ANOTHER STATE. THIS MEANS WE LITERALLY HAVE NO BEGINNING AND NO END. WE ARE ALWAYS ALIVE. (P.31)

6

IT IS SAID THAT A CIRCLE HAS NO BEGINNING OR END, BUT THIS IS NOT TRUE. A CIRCLES END IS ITS BEGINNING. WHILE THE CIRCLE IS BEING COMPLETED, THE BEGINNING AND END ARE VISIBLE, BUT, ONCE IT'S COMPLETE, END MEETS BEGINNING AND THEY DISAPPEAR. THIS IS THE VERY NATURE OF

LIFE. WHEN THE BODY DIES, END MEETS BEGINNING AND, THUS, BEGINNING AND END CANCEL EACH OTHER OUT, FOR THE LIFE AFTER THE DEATH IS THE SELF-SAME LIFE AS THE ONE BEFORE BIRTH. (P.31)

7

ONCE THE FLESH HAS BEEN SHED, THE SPIRIT-MIND IS FREED FROM THE LAWS AND FLAWS OF THE FLESH, SUCH AS DISABILITY AND DISEASE, AND IS RESTORED TO ITS FORMER GLORY IN PERFECTION, NO LONGER SUBJECT TO CORRUPTION OR LIMITATION AND IS FREE TO BECOME SUBJECT TO ITS OWN IMAGINATION, JUST LIKE IT IS WHEN WE DREAM. ONLY THE BODY DIES, WHILE THE SPIRIT-MIND REMAINS CONSCIOUS AND ALIVE. (P.32)

8

THE FLESH IS SIMPLY THE VEHICLE OUR SPIRIT-MIND CHOSE TO FULFILL THE PURPOSE OF ITS VISIT TO EARTH. IT IS ONLY THIS VEHICLE WHICH DIES, NOT THE DRIVER. IF I DROVE IN A CAR TO MEET MY WIFE, SHE WOULD GREET ME RATHER THAN THE CAR, FOR IT'S WHAT'S INSIDE THE CAR THAT IS THE REAL ME. ALSO, IF THE CAR BREAKS DOWN, I DO NOT BREAK DOWN WITH IT, BUT, INSTEAD, I GET OUT OF IT AND CONTINUE MY JOURNEY WITHOUT IT. EVEN THOUGH I MAY BE ASSOCIATED WITH THE CAR AND EVEN RECOGNIZED BY IT, IT IS NOT ME. I AM THE DRIVER WITHIN AND I AM MUCH LONGER-LASTING THAN MY VEHICLE. (P.35)

9

WHEN WE LOSE SOMEONE, WE SHOULD BE

MINDFUL OF THE FACT THAT THEY ARE STILL NEAR US, SO WE SHOULD BEHAVE HOW WE WOULD LIKE THEM TO SEE US BEHAVING, KNOWING THEY STILL LOVE US AND STILL WANT US TO BE HAPPY AND MAKE THE MOST OF OUR LIVES. KNOW THAT AS LONG AS WE ARE HAPPY, THEY ARE HAPPY. (P.36)

10
     WHEN THE SUN GOES DOWN, WE MISS IT, BUT WE CAN REST ASSURED OF OUR INEVITABLE REUNION WITH IT, IN THE LIGHT OF THE NEXT DAY. ONLY WE, WHO ARE LEFT BEHIND, KNOW THE DARKNESS OF NIGHT, BECAUSE FOR THE SUN ITSELF, IT IS AN ETERNAL DAY. THIS IS THE TRUE NATURE OF OUR LIVES. WHEN SOMEONE LEAVES THE FLESH, THEY ARE ONLY GONE FROM SIGHT, BUT WE DO SEE THEM AGAIN, IN THE LIGHT; THE SUN WILL NEVER KNOW NIGHT AND WE SHALL NEVER KNOW DEATH. (P.39)

11
     THERE'S NO END TO LIFE, <u>WE CAN LOOK FORWARD TO THE DAY WE SEE THEM AGAIN AND, IN THE MEANTIME, LIVE OUR LIVES TO THE FULL.</u> WE MUST REMIND OURSELVES THAT WHERE THEY ARE NOW, THEY ARE *LITERALLY* STILL ALIVE AND WELL. THEY ARE TRULY FREE. IT IS NEVER TOO LATE TO TALK TO THEM AS THEY CAN HEAR US WHENEVER WE SPEAK TO THEM, SO SPEAK TO THEM, SAY IT OUT LOUD, THEY WILL HEAR YOU. ALSO, DON'T THINK OF THEM BEING IN THEIR COFFIN FOR THEY ARE NOT IN THERE, AS THEY ARE NOT IN THEIR

BODY, MEANING THEY CAN BE NEAR US WHEREVER
WE ARE, JUST AS WE DON'T HAVE TO GO TO CHURCH
OR TEMPLE TO BE NEAR, OR TALK TO THE CREATOR.
(P.51)

12

FROM THE PERSPECTIVE OF THE SPIRIT-MIND,
THERE IS NO END TO, OR BREAK IN LIFE, JUST A
RETURN TO A HIGHER, FREER LEVEL OF
CONSCIOUSNESS; CONTINUOUS CONSCIOUSNESS; AN
ETERNAL, UN-INTERRUPTED LIFE. DEATH ONLY
EXISTS FROM THE BODY'S PERSPECTIVE, WHILE THE
PERSON(ALITY) WE KNOW AND LOVE LIVES ON
OUTSIDE THE BODY. WE COME FROM MIND AND
RETURN TO MIND, HAVING USED OUR BODY FOR THE
GAINING OF KNOWLEDGE AND, MOST IMPORTANTLY,
TO GAIN AND SHARE LOVE, FOR <u>LOVE IS THE ENERGY
OF ETERNAL LIFE. OUR WHOLE REASON FOR BEING IS
TO EXPERIENCE AND EXPRESS LOVE. THIS IS THE
MEANING OF LIFE.</u> (P.94)

I Give Thanks

I give thanks to the Most High Goddess, THE HOLY SPIRIT, for Love & All Creation!

I give thanks to Almighty JAH for Life, guidance, protection & inspiration.

I give thanks to Yahshuah for showing the Way to Salvation by example.

I give thanks to Emperor Haile Selassie I, King Alpha, for Revelation & for being the Lion of Judah who breaks every chain. JAH live.

I give thanks to Her Imperial Majesty, Empress Menen, for ever loving JAH.

I give thanks for my Queen, Bokhabinyana, and our beautiful little Princess, KaRa, for blessing my life & showing me the Glory of God/true Love! I love you both. I live you. See you when I get Home. *I miss you!* But I know you're here! XX

I give thanks for Marcus Mosiah Garvey, who prophesied of the coming of the Redeemer, the African King, the Lion of Judah; Ras Tafari.

I give thanks for Robert Nesta Marley & the myriad of talented Jamaican Reggae artists who teach us that we are one with JAH (I&I); that we are Nazarites (book of Numbers, Chapter 6, Bible); that Ras Tafari is the fulfilment of Bible prophecy & that we are all Kings & Queens; Sons & Daughters of JAH.

I give thanks for my parents, Rick & Sandy, for making me the person I am. Thank you mum for the gift & for being you. Thank you Dad for the signs you gave us that inspired much of this book & for the unique memories and experiences. I'm honoured and blessed to be your son.

I give thanks for my family, Jeannie, Keith, Mandy,

117

Karen, Doris, Brian, Andy, Petrina & family, grandma, granddad, Dot, Brenda, Lorna, David, Reel, Larry, Nonky, Sam, Mmemotswadi, Baba, Lefa, Kay, Kamo & Motheo, Thandi & Thando, Kguwi, "Ara," Shamme & Maborite family, Poshi & Lesedi, Mawe, Malume Mbix & Sakie & many more; you're all a blessings in my life, thank you.

I give thanks for my extended family; JAHson for saving my life, Shaun for brotherly love; Lisa & family; AndousJAHla & family; Victor, "P"& family; Roddie, Bones, Biggerman, Fabian, Noel, Rob "Zen," Massive; Tebza & Thuli for bringing such a wonderful Queen into my life & God-daughter Azania & Ruby; Romeo & Cynthia, Sis Karin & family; Sis Leah, Mau Mau & family; Sis Heather & Bro Dan; Sis Kerri, Mama B & the Knysna Rasses; Kebra; Kamo; Choma & family; "T", Jewels, Mel & Jim, Ous Tiny; Mangwane; Tshepi & family; Muzi, Solomon & family; Malcolm & family; Daisy, Chay & family; Saba, Arafayn & family; Sis Asher & family; Sis Benji & family; Dawn; Derry; Steve; Peace Man & Nicola, Presh & Nkosi; Paulette, Peter, Jennifer, JAHnine, Terry, Mushira, Obi; Ram & Bev; Adele; JAH Free & Sis Simiah; Tony & Rosie; JAH Waggy, Jake; Carly; Keety & Tabz; Reece, Benji; Duane; Shon & Nikki; Red-I & family; Sisa; Thabang, Sindi; Fani & the Durban crew; Johnny, Aminata, Carine, Felipe, Paul, Bheki, Tempa, Ellen, Clive, Loveness, Cyprian & Patricia, Thabo, Sis Ruthendo & many more for all the love! Thank you Richard for risking your life for my wife, bless you! I give thanks for all the Reggae sound men & women for one love vibes; and thank YOU so much for reading my book, I really hope it's helped.

WE ARE ALL ONE ETERNAL FAMILY!

Lightning Source UK Ltd.
Milton Keynes UK
UKHW02f1443260818
327821UK00006B/173/P